THE FAREHAM OF YESTERYEAR

Ron Brown

Down Memory Lane I linger long,
Till evening shadows fall,
To dream of golden days bygone,
And radiant hours recall.

Phototypesetting by Inforum Ltd, Portsmouth

Printed in Great Britain by
Conifer Press, Fareham, Hampshire

First Impression 1983
Reprinted 1985

British Library Cataloguing in Publication Data

Brown, Ron, *1932–*
    The Fareham of yesteryear.——2nd ed.——(Down memory lane; 13)
    1. Fareham (Hampshire)——Social life and customs
    I. Title   II. Series
    942.2'775   DA690.F224

    ISBN 0–903852–48–9

Peaceful Creek scene.

The elderly gent in the cloth cap ambled along the crowded pavement until he reached his destination, a glass-fronted establishment with two entrances, one sporting the title "Saloon Bar", the other "Public Bar". He entered the latter, pausing only to let the brown and white mongrel dog at his feet enter first.

"Morning Ted," offered the ruddy-faced man behind the bar, "Mondays certainly seem to come around quickly. Usual?." The old chap nodded and waited patiently for the glass of foaming liquid to pass across the counter, then on receiving it he shuffled over to a corner table. But the little dog remained at the base of the bar with eyes directed expectantly upwards. "Don't worry Toby, I haven't forgotten you," said the barman, producing a stone bowl and filling it with ale from the spillage trays beneath the pump handles. On having the bowl placed before him on the floor, Toby wagged his tail in sheer delight and began lapping at the beverage with great alacrity.

Within ten minutes, Ted was joined at his table by another regular Monday morning customer, his old friend Jim. "Hello Ted, having your market day usual I see." Ted nodded: "That's right Jim, I've left the wife traipsing around the market, women seem to get pleasure out of that sort of thing. As far as I am concerned, Fareham Market lost its appeal when they stopped the cattle auctions, it is just the people who get herded around like cattle now!"

As will generally happen when old chums get together, the conversation soon turned to sweet days of youth. "If those old-uns from when we were kids could come back and see the town as it is today, I should think that they would have a job to recognize the place! Cor, how it has changed, especially West Street, it is now more like Oxford Street," said Jim. "Sure enough," replied Ted, "It is a shame really, I know they say that you can't stand in the way of progress, but we did have some fine buildings and some great characters in the town that you and I grew up in. They are just memories now, and when we have passed on those old places and faces will be lost forever."

After another hour of reminiscing and sipping ale, the two old friends said goodbye and went their separate ways, each knowing that with advancing age their Monday meetings would soon be a thing of the past.

I heartily endorse their sentiments, it would be a shame if those memories of the Fareham of yesteryear were lost, for although it has emerged as one of the most progressive towns on the South Coast, only be delving back into the past can we gauge the progress that has been made.

I have to be honest, Fareham is the answer to a local historians prayers, for the simple reason that over the past twenty years or so it has undergone drastic physical change, thus emphasizing the comparison between old and new. In the following pages I will attempt through words and pictures to remind older readers of the Fareham that has passed, and hopefully charge younger readers with a measure of enthusiasm to record the history of the town they now live in, for they may well be the Teds and Jims of the next century. I will not go as far as to state that they will also meet on market days, for this institution will also probably be a thing of the past by then. Come to think of it, so might pubs!

Portland Hall, 1861.

West Street, c.1830.

EARLY BEGINNINGS

Nobody can be absolutely certain that the early Britons inhabited Fareham to any great extent, although various implements have been unearthed around the area. But, on the whole, the early tribes were not coastal types, much preferring to stick their "Shangri-la" plaques on their mudhuts in the Meon and Itchen Valley parts of the county. The chief reason for this was the availability of fresh water, so they made their settlements near streams surrounded by good pasture land for cattle.

Although they did not erect a motorway cafe at Fareham, it is certain that the Romans knew the place well, for it was on the route of their version of the M27 from Portchester to Venta Belgarum, via Clausentum. For readers who are not fortunate enough to own a chariot, I will explain that Venta Belgarum was the Roman name for Winchester, and Clausentum was the title they afforded to Bitterne near Southampton. So, if any drivers are not happy about some of the directional deviations on our roadway network of today, they should send their complaints on a postcard to Rome, for it was the Romans who originally determined and laid the foundations of our modern routing system.

The Danish Vikings found Fareham ideally suited for their vile purposes, allowing them to operate a form of roll-on-roll-off system for their excursions in the cause of rape and pillage. When one considers the enthusiasm with which both British and French day-trippers appear to attack each other's coastal ports and supermarkets via the cross-Channel ferry services of today, some readers might conclude that history has changed very little! Anyway, the ravaging that Fareham suffered at the hands of the Danes must have been serious, for we find that at the time of the Domesday Survey the Bishop of Winchester deemed that Fareham should have its taxes reduced because of the heavy damage incurred by the barbarian invaders. This meant that although Fareham contained 30 hides, it was assessed at 20.

Any reduction must have been very welcome, for many manors in Hampshire were subjected to heavy financial burdens. Before William the Conqueror's reign was over, Bishop Walkelin had begun the task of building the great Norman Cathedral at Winchester. Commencing in 1079, it was completed in 1093. Unfortunately, the Bishop must have made a slight miscalculation, for a few years later the great tower collapsed! Oh well, back to the drawing board! The tower rebuilding programme proved to be very costly, and the Domesday Book shows only too painfully how the money to pay the masonry and carpentry bills was raised. Meon was ordered to pay the Bishop £40 instead of their usual £30, Exton £30 instead of £20, and Fareham got off fairly lightly at £20 instead of £16.

At the time of the Domesday Survey Fareham was known as Fernham, but our forebears appeared to play games with E's and N's, and at various times it was called Ferham or Ferneham. One thing for sure, the latter syllable of the name, 'ham', denotes an Early Saxon occupation. The title of Fareham emerged around the 14th Century, thus ridiculing an old legend that it derived the name through a visit from Queen Elizabeth the First. The story goes that when Good Queen Bess was passing through the town one fine day, she was evidently so struck by the beauty surrounding it, she suggested that "Fairham" would be more appropriate than Fernham. But, whether it be called Fareham or Fernham, the town's close proximity to Farnham has created a good deal of confusion over the years. This will be verified by an army of long-distance lorry drivers, who after unloading a heavy consignment of goods on to the pavement outside premises in West Street, are informed: "Sorry mate, you have overshot by 30 miles, this delivery note says Farnham, you are now in Fareham." To which our husky driver friend no doubt replies: "Oh! dear me, what a Silly Billy I am!" Or something like that!

The Domesday Book in 1086 states that Fernham belongs to the Bishopric, and is possessed of a church, six slaves, two mills of the annual value of 25/-, plus ten hogs which would be turned out in the woods. In its early days, Fareham was probably nothing more than a hamlet under strict manorial rule. The good folk of Fareham were none too pleased at the antics of Bishop Henry de Elois, who in 1136 filched the Great Tithes from them in order to establish a "Hospital for Poor Brothers" in Winchester, better known as St. Cross. Although they did not have much love for Henry, they certainly had a great deal of respect for one of his successors, Peter de Rupibus, who became Bishop of Winchester in 1205. Popularly known as Peter des Roches, he set up a home in Fareham known as Roche Court. Although this residence paled somewhat against the large Bishop's Palace at Bishop's Waltham, it has still played a significant part in the history of Fareham, as we shall discover later.

One of Peter des Roches' successors, John de Pontissara, who was Bishop of Winchester from 1280 to 1304, had something of a windfall. This came about through King Edward the First, who on coming to the throne inherited land and property in Fareham. In 1284 he gave away all his rights and claim in the manor of Fareham to Bishop John and his successors in the Church. Around that period Fareham enjoyed the status of a mesne borough, and was described in early documents as the "Borough of Fareham". At the commencement of English Parliament, Fareham was one of the few towns in the county to send representatives to the early assemblies. This it did for the Parliament that met at Carlisle on January 20th, 1306, when as yet only Southampton, Winchester, Basingstoke, and Portsmouth shared that honour, or rather burden, of representation. Fareham's political influence was probably due to having the powerful De Borhunte and Brocas families in the neighbourhood.

Anyway, akin to many other towns in the country, Fareham could not afford to be represented in Parliament, and moves were made to opt out in the 1340s by means of a petition to King Edward the Third. On Sunday July the 2nd, 1345, the King was in the area preparing for a voyage to France, when John de Offord, the Dean of Lincoln, took the opportunity to deliver the Seal of Presence to the Keeper of the Privy Seal, and was pleased to receive the Seal of Assent for Fareham in return.

By the 14th Century, Fareham was beginning to establish its presence as a commercial port, an occurrence no doubt enhanced by Fareham Park with its many trees, being in close proximity to the town. Fareham Park was in existence from a very early date, for in 1279 complaints were recorded about certain persons breaking into Bishop's Park at Fareham and carrying away the deer, thus reminding us that Lincolnshire was not the only place associated with poaching. The Pipe Roll for 1323 records the wage paid to the keeper of the park, and the Court Rolls also provide various references relating to the park, including a payment of 3/4d. in 1477 to provide a hedge around it.

The timber in both Fareham and Titchfield Parks was in great demand for shipbuilding, and was generally transported to places such as Chatham by sea from Fareham or Warsash. The Victoria County History of England includes an interesting extract in respect of the park, this being in a letter sent by Sir Antony Windsor in 1538 to Lord Lisle, the Deputy of Calais and Sheriff of Hampshire. It reads: "As to your great wood you wrote for, there is a thousand ready tallied in Farahame Park and a thousand more shall be ready shortly, and then your warrant is expired. I would advise you to make suit to my Lord of Winchester to have a quantity of wood each year, for there is a new woodward, a servant of Sir William Paulet. Your Lordship will understand that by a sudden change of officers there will be secret enemies, and when the wrongdoers are tried it will be well to have a friend about the King''. Wow, a tale of intrigue indeed! The letter also informs that the deer poachers are still having a ball, and keeping the local folk well supplied with meat on the Black Market.

In 1636 Robert Rigge was acting as ''undertaker'' for Hampshire, this meant that he had the task of getting the required timber conveyed to the waterside. In 1637 Mr. Rigge was accused of cheating the carters, the fixed sum per load being 3/4d., of which he kept back 4d. Just to make matters worse, he was also charged with failing to repair the bridge at Fareham Quay. I should add that prior to its reputation in timber trading, Fareham also enjoyed some fame as a wine port in the 14th Century.

In 1638, the ''good men of Fareham'' were requested to supply the King, Charles I., with a ship of 400 tons complete with 160 men, to be ready at Portsmouth within four months. Regarding the ensuing Civil War, Fareham is reported to have been loyal to the King. The town paid for this affiliation in many ways, for it was seriously plundered by the Cromwellian forces at regular intervals. The Rev. G.N. Goodwin in his book of 1882, *The Civil War in Hampshire*, relates an incident that took place in January 1645, in which the Parliamentary army burnt down twenty or so houses in Gosport, then marched westwards, driving off all the cattle, horses, sheep, swine, and carrying away many men from Fareham and Titchfield.

Fareham's civic affairs were governed by the Borough Court for nearly 400 years, the first record of a court being in 1337, and from that date they were held almost continuously until 1729. The meetings took place in the Borough Market House, a quaint structure situated right in the middle of West Street, rather like the old Market House in Gosport High Street prior to 1814. At one time the Fareham mini-government comprised a Bailiff, two Constables, and two Ale-tasters! I should imagine that if the latter two gentlemen put in some overtime in the course of their work, some of the decisions that they reached in court could have been rather interesting!

A more stable climate in local affairs was reached in 1849 with the adoption of the Public Health Act in Fareham, when the governing of the town was vested in a Board of Health comprising nine members. The first election to provide members for the Local Board was conducted by Lord Henry Cholmondely, whose certificate of the result was dated 11th of October, 1849. The returning officer was Mr. J. Stedham, Clerk to the Guardians of Fareham Union. The election resulted in a keen contest, with 25 candidates fighting it out for the nine seats. The successful nine members were Richard Porter – merchant, Robert James – merchant, Alexander Dickson – Commander R.N., Joseph Paddon – gentleman, James James – brewer, George Garrett – gentleman, Henry Clark – merchant, John Hewett – gentleman, and Edward Turner – cooper and basket maker. Mr. Porter was elected Chairman of the Board, and James Taylor, who was also manager of the Gas Works and the Baths, was appointed as Clerk to the Board. Alfred Driver took this office over from Mr. Taylor in 1862, and when he died in 1883 he was succeeded by Leonard Warner, a well-known name in Fareham around the turn of the century.

The advent of the Local Board was just one of the many changes that took place in the first half of the last century. In 1800, Fareham was little more than a large village, chiefly comprising small houses and cottages, many of them thatched. The streets were unpaved, and cart horses were left tethered to rails outside dwellings. In fact, many of the buildings in the main thoroughfares were not much better than barns. As the population rose from

3,000 in 1800 to 5,800 by 1850, old buildings were pulled down and replaced by brick structures. The ancient and decrepit structures that had dominated the centre of West Street also received the attention of the demolition hammer, thus making this thoroughfare much wider than many of its counterparts in neighbouring towns, and influencing the development of West Street as a centre of commerce rather than the High Street.

In 1846, a small Market Hall was erected in West Street by subscription through £5 shares, the owners of which being allowed free admission. Within a short space of time, the hall was used as a Sunday School and as a church meeting room. But, in my view the most imposing building erected in West Street in that fifty year period just has to be the Portland Hall complex. The site was purchased by the Society for Literary and Philosophical Objects in 1834, and by the following year a splendid building in the Ionic style was adorning the corner position. It was a proud moment for the President of the Society, the Rev. Sir Henry Thompson, when the institute was officially opened by Lord Brougham, who was Lord Chancellor at one time. The hall was much appreciated by Fareham residents in its early years, the most popular events proving to be the enthusiastic debates that took place on the works of Shakespeare.

The building was sold in 1858 and taken over by the Local Board as a Town Hall, with various positions of the building let to local organizations for a variety of functions. In fact, throughout its history, the building has played many roles, housing Fareham Post Office at one time, and also the Savings Bank. It was also the meeting place for the Fareham Choral and Dramatic Societies, the Band of the Royal Marines were regular visitors for concerts, and that great attraction of the age, Mrs Jarley's Waxworks and Tableaux Virants, drew large crowds to the hall.

The outside of the Portland Hall provided the arena for many exciting election scenes in bygone years, and in my postcard collection I appear to have accumulated quite a number of pictures of Lord Arthur Lee and his good lady acknowledging the cheers of their supporters as it was announced that he had held the South Hants seat for the Conservatives yet again. Of course, this was in the days when the Liberals and the Tories were the main parties, for Keir Hardie and his Labour boys had not as yet got up steam. In his first battle for the seat in Gosport and Fareham, Arthur Lee had to fight it out against a Liberal gentleman named Tweedy-Smith. Mr. Tweedy-Smith's undoing proved to be his enthusiasm for the new-fangled horseless carriage, an invention that was not looked upon too favourably by the local farmers. Our Liberal friend made the mistake of driving his fume-belching and spluttering iron monster around the local countryside, scaring the wits out of the farmers, horses and cattle alike! On the other hand, being no fool, our Arthur did his canvassing by pony and trap. Needless to say, he won the seat and doubled the Conservative majority!

To be nearer his constituents, Arthur and Ruth Lee rented the great house at Rookesbury Park, Wickham, and at one time his mother lived in Fareham, at No. 12 in the High Street. He also owned a large property known as Chequers, and towards the end of the First World War, when Arthur was enjoying a friendly period with Lloyd George, he presented Chequers to the nation for the use of future prime ministers. It was through his affinity with the Liberals, and his verbal skirmishes with Lord Charles Beresford, Winston Churchill, and Campbell-Bannerman, that he was dismissed from the local political scene when the Tories took over from the Liberals in 1922. Arthur Lee was made a peer, thus ending the long service that he had given to the people of Fareham and Gosport.

A final word on elections in Fareham, one of the most exciting events during the hustings took place long before the arrival of Arthur Lee, this was when Sir F. Fitzwygram and Captain Wilber-

Market Hall and Price's School.

The Bank, West Street.

force were in competition for the electors' votes. Fitzwygram was addressing a large crowd outside the Portland Hall whilst standing in his carriage, when one of his opponent's supporters cut the reins and caused the team of horses to bolt off through the crowd, creating instant pandemonium and bringing that politician's speech to an abrupt finish! The rotten devils!

During alterations in later years at Portland Hall, writing was discovered on a beam by workmen, it informed that gas had been brought into the building on 19 August, 1836. This early example of graffiti was signed by W. Faro and G. Silverlock. It must have been one of the first gas installations, for the gas works was established in that same year at a cost of £3,800 by a company of shareholders. The Fareham streets were lit by the wonder of gas, a great boon indeed to the town's inhabitants. The popularity for domestic gas appliances had increased considerably by the end of the century, and so a showroom and offices for the Fareham Gas & Coke Company was opened in West Street, next to the Crown Inn. The Fareham gas undertaking was taken over by the Gosport District Gas Company in 1925, bringing glad tidings to the Fareham users, for the price of gas was almost halved. In the 1930s the name was changed yet again, to the Portsmouth & Gosport Gas Company, which it kept until nationalization after the war.

By the time of the Second World War, that other source of power known as electricity had been established in Fareham around fifty years. I have read that Fareham was the first place in the country to have its streets lit by electricity, but this is not entirely correct, for that honour must go to Godalming in Surrey. Three electric street lamps were erected and lit in Godalming in 1881, the current being generated by water power. It was a huge success, attracting spectators by the hundreds to view this truly amazing spectacle. The obvious step to take next was to light all of Godalming's streets by electricity, but the gas undertaking fought hard to retain control, and the good people of Godalming had to wait until 1897 until their streets were entirely lit by electricity. Electric street lighting was introduced to Fareham in 1890, and the town may rightly claim to be the first in the country to have its streets wholly lit by this source of power. There are still a number of early lamp-posts to be found in Fareham, especially in the High Street, where those dated 1897 to commemorate Queen Victoria's Diamond Jubilee are of particular interest.

An electricity generating station was in operation from Lower Quay until 1932, although the Southern Electricity Board retained stores and offices there until 1976, the arrival of the M27 motorway allowing it to base its services from Drayton. I expect many local people will recall the old electricity showroom in West Street, next to Westbury Manor, where Charlie Horner was in charge. The corner premises are now occupied by an estate agent.

In this modern age we rely greatly on the resources of both gas and electricity, in fact it would be difficult to imagine what life would be like without them, but of course there is another need that is even more important, the need for water. In the old days it was a case of dropping a bucket down a well, that is if you were lucky enough to have or live near a well. For those who were not so fortunate, you had to obtain your supply of water from the parish pump that was situated near the old Market House in West Street. Waterworks were established in Fareham in 1859, and the early guidebooks go to great lengths to inform their readers that the Fareham water supply is second to none, of excellent purity, and could no doubt reach parts that no other water will reach!

Although water is marvellous for drinking and keeping clean, in olden days it was also used as a form of punishment, that novel piece of equipment known as a ducking stool springing immediately to mind. However, the most common form of punishment was provided by the stocks, with the wrongdoer forced into being a sitting target and subjected to missiles such as rotten fruit or eggs. The stocks in Fareham were used well into the last century, one set could be found near the Red Lion Hotel, whilst another set was situated on the corner of Osborn Road.

Of course, just a rotten tomato's throw away from the stocks in Osborn Road, in later years there was an official law and order establishment in the form of the old police station. This building functioned until 1980, when the Boys in Blue of the Hampshire Constabulary moved lock, stock, and handcuffs into their magnificent new police station in Quay Street. The old building in Osborn Road is still in use for dealing out sentences, for it now serves as a Register Office!

The first police station in Fareham was erected in 1854 at a cost of £250, and a few years later a courtroom was added for £130, a sum that was raised by voluntary contributions from the magistrates, who held Petty Sessions there on alternate Mondays. The strength of the Fareham force at that time was one Superintendent, David Harvey, and three constables, this number steadily increasing with the town's population figures. The law enforcers of Fareham gained considerable status in 1924 when the Gosport force was amalgamated with them to form the Fareham Division. Superintendent William Jacobs was put in charge of the much larger division, and he was followed a few years later by Superintendent Walter Jones. I wish that I had space to mention more police personnel from the past, but I am afraid that we shall have to finish on Tom Drew, who was Fareham Superintendent of police in the last century. Tom was very well thought of in the town, and when he died in 1872 it was undoubtedly the funeral of the year, with almost the whole town turning out to say farewell. It was a most impressive affair indeed, the kind that would make the undertakers of today drool at the mouth. The pall bearers included four superintendents, and eight constables. Tom must have been a big chap!

Before the telephone made such an intrusion into our lives, folk used to keep themselves well occupied with letter writing, thus providing plenty of work for the postal services. In earlier times Fareham was well served with mail, many horse-drawn coaches called there, with Portsmouth and Southampton to the east and west respectively, and Gosport to the south. In the middle of the last century there was a post office at Mr. Augustus Nicholson's establishment in West Street, although his main business concern was that of a bookseller. By this time, the wonders of rail travel had reached Fareham, and letters were despatched by rail to all parts twice a day. The White's Directory for 1859 lists James Nicholson and Henry Hale as letter carriers, whilst William Ventham acted as village postman, so he must have possessed the toughest feet of this postal trio.

In the early part of this century the Fareham Post Office was sited close to where Messrs. Woolworth's are now, more or less opposite the top of Portland Street. Norman Stedman was the popular postman there, and the office was open for business from 8 a.m. until 7 p.m.. The post office moved in later years further down West Street to face the top of Hartlands Road, then in the 1960s it moved to the palatial new office it now occupies a few doors away.

Mr. Welling took over from Mr. Stedman as Fareham Postmaster in 1919, and remained until 1925, when he left to become postmaster at Petersfield. One of his successors at Fareham, George Jackson, did a great deal to re-organize and improve the town's postal service. It is interesting to recall that when he was away from the post office counter, George made quite a name for himself by writing books for boys. George Jackson died in 1935 at the age of 58, and his place as postmaster was taken by Mr. E. Beck. Whenever a postman retired in years gone by, the local newspapers were sure to produce a plethora of facts and figures about how many letters he had delivered, or how many miles he had tramped in his postal career. Solomon Richards has to be included in these statistics, for he delivered the mail around Fareham for 45 years, starting as a messenger boy in 1881. It was estimated that he had walked several times around the world! Ouch! my aching feet!

Another milestone in the town's affairs came in 1894, this was when the Board of Health disappeared under the Local Government Act, and was replaced by the Fareham Urban District Council. The honour of being the first Chairman of the F.U.D.C. went to John Sandy, a well known character who was born in Fareham in 1859. He also served on Hampshire County Council, and was a magistrate in the town from 1907. John was a staunch Liberal, and in 1910 he had the courage to take on Arthur Lee in the Parliamentary elections.

The old Westbury Manor was in use as council offices for many years, which reminds me of an amazing incident that took place in the early 1960s, in fact it was on a Monday morning that followed a weekend in which the clocks had to be altered for Summertime. It also happened to be April the First, a date that did not go unmarked by a young assistant in the adjacent Electricity Board showroom. During a quiet period he reached up and put the showroom clock on from 11 o'clock to 12, then went behind a partition and produced sandwiches from his case. The unsuspecting shop manager, Fred Day, was behind the partition doing paperwork, he queried the time on the wall clock with his wristwatch, only to be told that he must forgotten to alter it with the time change. "My Goodness" said Fred, "It is lunchtime, I had better get some water for a cup of tea".

Now, this is how jokes can have a nasty habit of snowballing. The electricity showroom did not have a supply of water on the premises, so water for a cup of tea had to be fetched from the nearby council offices in Westbury Manor. Fred Day hurried into the Manor with his kettle and washing-up bowl, and on seeing that the clock in the entrance hall registered 11 a.m., he laughingly informed the council receptionist that they too had forgotten to put the clocks on at the weekend. She immediately went into action, exclaiming "Oh! dear, they should be at lunch now", and sounded the lunch alarm! Still chuckling, Fred returned to the showroom with his water. On looking up at the clock, which in the meantime had been set back to 11 a.m., realization suddenly dawned! He just had time to utter "You ******'s", and was last seen speeding back to Westbury Manor in order to try and stop the council workers, who were never ones to miss an opportunity from going to lunch at 11 o'clock instead of 12!

But, I digress, we must get back to earlier times. In the following pages I will attempt to remind readers about some of the events, characters, and establishments that have played their part in the shaping of Fareham's history.

Milling Around

After reading accounts of various council meetings, I feel some folk might come to the conclusion that mud-slinging is accepted as normal within chamber walls. In the Fareham of yesteryear, mud-slinging was indeed a popular pastime, but with real mud! On the Eve of St. Peter's Day every year, the mill pond was drained of water and all and sundry had the right to search for eels and other fish on the mud flats. It is not difficult to imagine what happened when several pairs of eyes alighted on a big juicy eel at the same time, a new meaning was brought to the expression "Here's mud in your eye".

I mentioned earlier that the Domesday Book included two mills at Fareham, and most certainly one of these was the old tidal mill situated on what was then the main Portsmouth Road. Every day the site of the old mill is passed by thousands of motorists approaching the Delme Roundabout, and despite a plaque recording its former presence, I very much doubt if half of those

West Street, 1906.

Cams Mill, by Martin Snape.

Peel Common Windmill in full sail.

Cams Mill.

Peel Common Mill before demolition.

15

who pass by have the slightest idea that a picturesque old mill once graced this spot.

There is no doubt that in early times the mill was an important feature in the Bishop's manorial rights, but by the beginning of this century it had declined into an antiquated structure that served very little purpose commercially. Having said that, I ought to add that the old tarred wooden building was the delight of artists and those who practised the up-and-coming art of photography. In its latter years the mill was known locally as "Clarke's Mill" by generations of Fareham folk. At one time it was owned by Montague Foster, that well known gentleman from Stubbington House. But sadly, by the outbreak of the First World War the mill was in a very bad state of repair, and although the local people were sorry to see it go, it was eventually demolished. That was the bad news, the good news is that there are plenty of paintings, sketches, and photographs of the old mill in existence to maintain a pictorial record.

By turning our backs on the sluice-gates at Delme and returning back down the creek to the Quay area, we would have found another flourishing mill, driven by steam rather than water. The large millhouse at Lower Quay was erected in 1830 by Thomas Burrell, and the mill was operated by four pairs of stones driven by a 45 h.p. beam-type steam engine. This method was replaced by roller mills in the 1880s, and in the following years when the business was in the hands of the Heasman family it underwent several modernization programmes. The large quayside building was in fact the first in the town to be electrified. This steam mill played an important part in the commercial world of Fareham for 130 years, and it was a sad day when milling ceased in 1960.

Well, so far we have touched upon one mill driven by water power, another by steam, so I think we ought to close this section by recalling the power of wind, yes, those revered structures known as windmills.

Within living memory, the nearest windmill to Fareham was situated to the south of the town, in Newgate Lane. As one approached Peel Common, a bungalow bearing the name Mill House will be found on the right hand side of the lane, this is one of the few reminders that a windmill once graced the landscape from this site. Standing in open farmland, the mill could be seen from many miles around. Most of the surrounding land was owned by Farmer Holliday of Rome Farm.

The kennels of the Gosport and Fareham Beagles were housed nearby, and many hunts started from the old mill in the early part of this century. After it ceased operations as a mill, the structure spent several years as a beerhouse, which was appropriately named the Windmill Inn. The windmill was demolished in 1926, and the bricks were used for the erection of a house close by known as Rowner Villa. A garage and Jack Harman's upholstery factory replaced the mill, and I have particularly fond memories of one visit I made to the site in the 1970s, for Jack Harman was able to show me the original mill stones from the windmill. The most common stones used for milling were imported from quarries in the Paris Basin, they were known as French Burr stones and were particularly suitable for grinding fine flour.

A mile or so away as the crow flies, there was another windmill in Crofton, but I do not wish to stray very far away from Fareham, for reasons that I will explain later. But for those readers who are old windmill addicts, and I know that there are quite a number, I would recommend another book in the **Down Memory Lane** series, *The Windmills of Hampshire* by Anthony Triggs.

Making A Living In Fareham

Before the demon bricklayers turned their trowels and attention in the direction of Fareham, the area sported many small farms, and at one time sheep-rearing was a very important local industry, but this has long since died out. However, well into this century many Fareham folk were content to make their living by working down on the farm, and what a wonderfully idyllic existence it must have been, breathing in lashings of unpolluted air and enjoying great hunks of crusty bread and cheese, the hearty appetites no doubt encouraged by many hours of shovelling "you know what" in the cowshed!

I have not enough space to mention all of them, but here are a few names from Fareham's farming past. In the last century we had Farmer Fred Burrell of Earles Farm, Bill Collier of Gudge Heath Farm, Tom Burrell of Alders Farm, Jim James of Charity Farm, James Martin of East Cams Farm, John Cooper of Maylands Farm, William Sandles of Crockerhill Farm, John Stares of Catisfield Farm, Jim Thresher of Fareham Park Farm, George Mansfield of White Dell Farm, and Bob Page of Albany Farm. Moving into this century we had Arthur Cole of Coombe Farm, Fred Hedges of Hellyers Farm, William Hill of Down Barn Farm in North Wallington, Lionel Adams of Red Barn Farm, Sam Holliday of Brook Farm off Gudgeheath Lane, Jim Wassell of Furze Hill Farm, and Tom Pond had taken over Albany Farm, Ernie West had Alders Farm, Walter Ireston had Blackbrook Farm, and Sydney Pink had White Dell Farm.

Of course, the obvious name is missing from the above is that of Tom Parker, the Dairy King who died in 1982 at the age of 86. A member of a long-established farming family, Tom Parker had farmed since the age of 14, and started business on his own account by taking over Charity Farm off the Wickham Road, then Heytesbury Farm at Crockerhill and Spurlings Farm in North Fareham. An astute businessman, he built an empire that covered 4,000 acres, specializing in the dairy side of farming where over 2,300 gallons of milk are produced daily and a packing station handles 180,000 eggs per day. Although the "Guv'nor" is no longer with us, the name of Tom Parker is still displayed proudly on milk floats and dairy shops around the area.

In the early part of this century there were quite a number of small market gardeners in Fareham. John Coker, who died in 1925 at the age of 79, was one of this happy band, and his vegetable cart pulled by a donkey was a familiar site in the streets of the town. Another well known name in this field was that of Drover, for this family ran the Royal Nurseries in Trinity Street for many years. William Drover inherited the business from his father, and his son William took over from him. They were famous all over the country for their prize chrysanthemums, and such was their fame that they supplied bouquets and sprays by Royal Appointment, delivering them to the Gosport Railway Jetty for Queen Victoria's pleasure, or even taking them personally to Osborne House on the Island. The last William Drover, who died in 1963 at the age of 78, developed an orchid which he named "Princess Beatrice".

Of course, whilst our hungry farmworkers scoffed the aforementioned bread and cheese during their lunch-breaks, it is quite likely that they washed it down with that refreshing liquid that is obtained from a beer bottle. It is also more than likely that the bottle had 'H.H. & R.J. Saunders' emblazoned on it, reminding us of that remarkable little brewery operating in North Wallington. I have an old Wallington Brewery bottle in my collection, and I try not to delve too long on the fact that in those days one dozen bottles of pale ale or stout cost only half-a-crown. Saunders also had the answer to keeping out the winter cold, this came in the form of a half-pint bottle of liquid dynamite that was afforded the title of Stingo Ale. A couple of these and one was immediately oblivious to cold, heat, or even the human race! Henry Saunders, who began the Wallington Brewery, died in 1900 at the age of 64.

Henry Saunders father was a well known local potter, and he had his works on the road that led to Fort Fareham. Thomas

Stares of Wallington established the first pottery in Fareham for the manufacture of chimney pots, flower pots, pans and pipkins. Other earthenware manufacturers include Richard Kiln of Wallington, Charles Smith of Old Turnpike, and George Harris of the Fareham Pottery. Mate's *1905 Guide to Hampshire* informs readers that a visit to the Fareham Pottery is well worth while, on account of the many beautiful objects in terra-cotta that were made there, especially the models from the antique reproductions of Egyptian and Cypriots jars, lamps, and vases. Another product to emerge from the Fareham Pottery works in great quantities were drain-pipes, but of course these were by no means as attractive as pots or vases to intending visitors to the works.

Still more or less on the same theme, I feel that it would now be opportune to mention another industry for which Fareham has some claim to fame, that of brick-making. The art of making bricks has flourished in Fareham for over two hundred years, although the excellence of the local clay for such a purpose was recognized several hundred years prior by our old friends the Romans. It is rather strange to reflect that the old brickworks were used to eventually create a monster that would eventually devour themselves, for many of the brickfield sites in Fareham were used for housing development from the 1920s onward. Brickyards existed at one time in West Street, near the railway station. and in the Gordon Road area, Holly Grove, Redlands Lane, Crockerhill, Furzehill, Wallington, and Fareham Common. Some of the names associated with the older brickfields include Stephen Burrell, Frederick Stares, Matthew Tate, William Cawte, William Oliver, James Wettam, John Pink, and James Smith

The quality of local bricks known as Fareham Reds was renowned throughout the world, and they were used for the building of many famous edifices, including the Town Hall in Cape Town, South Africa. On a local note they were used for the construction of the many forts surrounding Fareham in the last century, for the railway viaducts at Bridgefoot and the Quay, several houses in the historic High Street, the bus station, and even the Embassy cinema in West Street. Up until the commencement of the last war in 1939, the brickyard in Funtley was a hive of industry, and for many local people it was a way of life, passed on from father to son, rather like miners. Even before the war there was competition in evidence from foreign brickmakers, and the Funtley yard closed just after the war. Looking at the site today, with the M27 motorway in the background, the site is desolate and certainly shows no signs of its former glory. It has also been the subject of rows about the future of the site in recent times, for it has obviously attracted the attention of building developers. So once again it could be a case of dog eat dog, or brick taking over brick.

Readers may have noticed that the tiny hamlet of Wallington is beginning to creep more and more into our story of Fareham, and it is there where we look for our next local industry, Wallington Tannery. One of the earliest names connected with this tannery is that of Rolfe, with William Rolfe getting the business off the ground in the 17th Century. Through marriage, the tannery eventually passed into the hands of the Thresher family, then in the 19th Century the business was acquired by Edward Sharland, who came from Devon to reside in Fareham.

White's 1859 guide lists Edward and Henry Sharland as tanners and bank merchants, and the horse-drawn carts loaded with hides or bark were a regular feature on the roads of Fareham, travelling back and forth between Fareham Railway Station and the Wallington Tannery. The tannery provided regular employment for quite a number of workers, and when the bark harvest was in full swing many extra men were taken on to cope with the work load. Although the wage was by no means marvellous, at least it was fairly regular, so it is understandable that it came as a terrible blow to local folk when the tannery eventually closed around 1910.

So far we have covered farming, brewing, brick and pottery making, and tanning. If we add to this minor industries such as boat building, rope and sail-making, and coach building, readers will be provided with some idea as to how the residents of Fareham past made their living. A final word on the latter trade, coach building, for Messrs. Coles employed at least thirty hands in their West Street factory in the last century. It was indeed a most successful business, for they exported carriages all over the world, even as far as Australia. The Coles could claim royal patronage, George III is reputed to have had the royal carriage wheels greased there, and William IV and Queen Victoria were pleased to call upon their services at various times, hence the Royal Arms proudly displayed over the premises. There was always a good selection of coaches or carriages arrayed outside the West Street factory, and whenever the annual fair took place you could be sure that there would always be friction between the Coles family and visiting showmen, with the latter complaining that Coles took up most of the highway with their wares. One such case went to court, it ended with Messrs. Coles being found guilty of having their carriages and wheels obstructing the road and causing a nuisance. They were ordered to remove the obstructions within seven days, and if they failed to comply with this they would be fined 60 shillings. Of course, with the coming of the railway traders such as Coles gradually became redundant, and the work-force had to turn their skills to other things.

Marketdays and Fairdays

I expect most readers will be familiar with the old adage "All work and no play", and although the workers of yesteryear did not have the attractions of television or bingo inflicted upon them in those days, they gained their pleasures in simple forms, such as fairs, or throwing mud at each other in the creek. As far as Fareham was concerned, the big days to look forward to in the year were the 29th and 30th of June, for this heralded St. Peter's Fair. Apart from acting as a venue where much horse-trading and price-haggling took place, this event was also the largest cheese fair in the country.

At times the fair was so vast it overflowed from West Street into the High Street, and as it was also a pleasure fair, swings and roundabouts adorned this noble thoroughfare. Try to imagine this scene in the last century, stalls stacked high with many varieties of cheeses, and with glass and crockery from which young couples could choose in the pleasure of making their first home. Other stalls sold toys, sweets, gingerbreads, cloths and ribbons etc., And all the while there was the happy excitement of parents and children partaking of the roundabouts and coconut shies, or the peep-show that was situated near the Red Lion Hotel. There was even a roundabout outside the hairdressing establishment of Mr. Quick in the High Street, although with such a distraction I don't think that I personally would fancy receiving a close shave at the hands of this demon barber!

In its heyday the fair spilled over into the churchyard and adjoining land, with cattle being kept in the churchyard and in Lady Bennett's Field. if anyone was still sober enough, or had sufficient energy, a grand regatta was always held on the river or creek to bring the merriment to a close. But, those were the good times for the fair, the bad times were close at hand. The fair held in Fareham in 1860 was reported to be the dullest for many years, there were very few horses for sale, and those that were available were awfully expensive. It was also noted that only a small number of cheese stalls were pitched, and it appeared that this branch of the fair was dying out rapidly. It continued until 1871, and that was the year that the annual Fareham fair for the Patron Saints of St. Peter and Paul was abolished. Hard Cheese!

Mind you, the residents of Fareham still had the occasional travelling show or fair to look forward to. On one such visit in

West Street, 1906. Kings Arms on right.

East Street, Red Lion.

West Street, west end.

East Street.

The Old Post Office, 1906.

Fareham Market.

New Post Office.

Fareham Market, sheep pens.

1887 there were fun and games that the show people did not bargain for. The show had a menagerie of tame and untamed animals of various species, and it was during a performance that a large brown bear escaped from its keeper. With spectators fleeing in all directions, the huge animal climbed a tree outside Mistletoe House in the High Street. Despite the efforts of the showmen and the local constables, the bear would not come down, and they had to wait until he was hungry enough to return to earth on his own accord!

Animals of a more docile nature could be seen regularly at Fareham Market, a weekly event that has flourished for many centuries. The market site that we are familiar with now is relatively new, for over sixty years ago it was held in West Street, with cattle and merchandise displayed in the road and on the pavements. With a variety of animals on view, Fareham took on the appearance on a Wild West cattle town, with cows, pigs, and sheep being herded down West Street from the railway station. Although it was a fairly common sight to see cattle roaming the main streets, some Fareham folk took exception to this practice, and in 1907 Farmer George Baker of Cams Alders Farm was summoned for allowing 20 cows to stray in Newgate Lane. Matters came to a head in 1925 when several complaints were made about the driving of pigs down West Street, the tram crews being particularly upset about delays caused by obstruction from animals blocking the highway. Some improvement took place when the market was moved out of West Street and into the marketyard, at least it relieved some of the congestion in the street. The move to the yard was brought about by the Market Company, which had been formed in the 1890s by a group of local farmers, and was controlled by Messrs. Austin & Wyatt the auctioneers and estate agents in the High Street.

The market was originally held on Wednesdays, but by the middle 1800s this had been changed to Mondays, as it is today. In the old days it was not only cattle that farmers haggled over, for wheat, grain and vegetable products were also on offer. Records in 1820 report that samples of wheat were in abundance, but at £18 per load there were no takers, it being the general opinion that because of the excellent quality and quantity of the harvest that year, wheat prices would be low. Which all rather smacks of the Common Market!

It is difficult now to imagine cattle being paraded and sold outside the Portland Hall, but back in the last century this was a reality. The stanchions and chains for the animals were placed in position by an old chap named "Sooty Doe", who combined the market business with his other job as a chimney sweep in the town. In the 1870s there was usually a Recruiting Officer for the Militia in attendance on marketdays, trying to entice suitable young chaps to sign on. He was the object of derision for the local youngsters, who would cheekily chant rhymes such as "Soldiers half-a-crown, Sailors half-a-guinea, Militia four-a-penny"!

Occasionally, the exciting market scene at Fareham was made even more exciting by an animal going beserk. One such incident in the 1930s was very memorable, this was when a bull belonging to Farmer Charlie House went mad and broke free from its handlers, charging off to leave behind it a trail of devastation. The chief objective of most people in the vicinity was to get out of the way as soon as possible, for I am afraid no matter how many times you utter "Heel" or "Stay" to a bull, it is not likely to take much notice, although the distinctive tones of Barbara Woodhouse might prove an exception!

With a definite shortage of Fareham matadors about that day, the bull was able to escape from the confines of the market and run down Quay Street into the recreation ground, where it romped around and eluded all attempts to capture it. It ran into Bath Lane and made its way back into West Street, its appearance prompting pedestrians to create records for climbing up lamp-posts. It then proceeded down to Kings Road, where it unfortunately impaled itself on some iron railings, making the poor creature even madder. Bellowing loudly, it charged into the nearby allotments, where Mr. Ward, a local Justice of the Peace, was doing a spot of gardening. Without prompting, Mr. Ward jumped into his shed; which took a hefty battering from the bull's horns. The J.P. was trapped in the shed for over an hour, until eventually a butcher named Nash was summoned to the scene, producing a gun he put the unfortunate animal out of its misery. No doubt our friend in the shed was also greatly relieved, in more ways than one!

Although the cattle auctions ceased in the early 1970s, the market at Fareham is still a popular venue every Monday, although in recent years there have been threats of closure, with the site being proposed for commercial development. Departmental stores have even been mentioned. Time will tell.

Pleasures were simple in the old days, with the spectacle of energetic young men attempting to climb the greasy pole proving to be a top attraction. The poles were erected in the middle of West Street, and if any of the contestants were nimble enough to reach the top of the pole, their prize was usually a leg of mutton. This was always good for a laugh, and so were some of the antics that many people in earlier times indulged in to win the wager. In 1809 a Mr. Blanchard of Gosport made a bet of 100 guineas that his mare could trot from Gosport to Chichester and back in under six hours. The horse was making reasonably good time, but unfortunately on the return journey of the sixty-mile trip the poor animal dropped dead from exhaustion when it reached Fareham.

More free street entertainment was provided in April 1860, when a young man named Pink, who was a shipwright at Haslar Gunboat Yard, undertook for a few shillings a wager to walk from Gosport to Fareham in under one hour, which he actually succeeded in completing in 52 minutes. But this pales beside the feat of a bricklayers' labourer in 1861, who for a bet of 25 shillings attempted to walk 100 miles in 24 hours. He actually accomplished the walk with half an hour to spare, stepping it out from Fareham to Gosport and back ten times. But the prize for the most unusual walk connected with Fareham must go to Norman Carter, who in 1937 walked from his lodgings in Fayre Road to Stubbington in the dead of night. So what was so unusual about Norman's midnight hike, well, the fact was that he did not know anything about it, he was sleepwalking! With bare feet, and clad only in his pyjamas, he must have tramped the four miles through the villages of Peel Common and Stubbington, and would probably still be walking if he had not been spotted by an early morning motorist. The motorist alerted P.C. Harvey, who very carefully woke Norman up. Imagine his surprise when he saw the Stubbington countryside instead of his comfy little bedroom!

Folk always appeared eager to attempt the impossible in days gone by, and tasks such as trundling a cartwheel around the world, or walking backwards around Great Britain were undertaken with relish. In 1926 the people of Fareham turned out to see film actor Harry Lorraine ride through the town on his motorbike, this was for the stage between Southampton and Portsmouth of his 6,000 mile ride around the United Kingdom, his object being to win a £500 wager made by a London club owner. Before readers begin thinking that this must have been easy money, I must add that Harry was handcuffed and manacled to the machine, and that he had to change speed by using his teeth!

So there we are, what with the fairs, markets, and endless parade of exhibitionists adding colour to our main thoroughfares, I harbour a notion that our streets had more life in them in the old days than they have today. One last thought on this subject, I am rather surprised that nobody has attempted to re-introduce the old-style street fair in Fareham, similar to the Free Mart Fair that has been brought back annually in Portsmouth with such great success. Just think of it, colourful stalls and attractions with people dressed in old costumes, and a maypole and roundabouts for the kids. The traffic would not be a problem, for with most of it skirting the main town area, West Street and the High Street could easily be transformed into a pedestrian precinct for one day. Just one thing, don't ask me to climb a greasy pole!

Going to Church in Fareham.

Crash! Miss Abraham stopped in her tracks, the sound of glass breaking came from the direction of the church building that she had just left. As organist at the parish church of S.S. Peter and Paul in Fareham, she had just cleared up her music sheets and was on her way home, the evening service had long since finished. On hearing the sound of the glass breaking, Miss Abraham summoned up the courage to investigate, for only the week before some ninety panes of glass had been broken by vandals at the Infants School. As she drew closer to the church, she could hear howling and shrieking coming from within, then suddenly a clear yell of "Let me out" filled the air. It turned out that the calls of distress were those of a young servant girl, who had fallen asleep during the sermon, and had somehow remained unseen by the other parishioners as they left the church. On waking and finding herself in the dark, the poor girl had a bout of hysterics. In her 27 years as organist at the church, it was quite the most frightening moment of Miss Abraham's musical career.

The above incident happened in 1875, and it is just one of the many stories associated with this historic church. Sitting proudly on one of the highest points of the town, this church once dominated the Fareham landscape, but in more recent years it has been dwarfed by the new Manhattan-style Civic Offices.

The church in Fareham mentioned in the Domesday Survey was probably quite a small structure, although sufficiently large enough to cater for the town's worshippers at that time. In addition to its religious function, situated as it was on the top of a hill, the building also served as an excellent lookout point for likely invaders, commanding outstanding views across the creek and harbour. The church building was gradually enlarged, and the oldest portion that can still be seen is occupied by the Old Chancel, probably dating from the 13th Century. The most dramatic physical change occurred in 1742, this being when the Georgian-style tower was added. With the tower came the traditional sound of bells, six of them at first, then in 1883 two more were added to provide a complete octave.

The nave of the church, a structure of red brick in the square style of the third George, was rebuilt in 1812, and consecrated two years later. In 1888, a new chancel was built in the Early English style, the old 13th Century chancel being restored as a side chapel. A vestry and organ chamber were also added at the same time. The *Victorian County History* was rather ungracious in its description of S.S. Peter and Paul, stating that although the church was exceedingly spacious and well adapted for preaching, it was distinctly unattractive as a building. To add insult to injury, it also implies that the designs from which it was built were originally intended for a silk factory. The 1812 nave was rebuilt in 1931 under the architectural direction of Sir Charles Nicholson, the end result being the splendid building that we know today.

One of the most colourful names connected with this church in the last century just has to be that of the Rev. Walter Scott Dumergue, a respected Vicar who was in fact the godson of Sir Walter Scott. Anyway, Mr. Dumergue was well loved by his flock at S.S. Peter and Paul, and a handsome alabaster pulpit was erected to his memory. Moving on into this century, I expect many older residents of Fareham will have fond memories of the Rev. James Tarbat, who was Vicar from 1901 to 1928. I am afraid when James Tarbat first came to S.S. Peter and Paul he did not have a very happy reception, for his first sermon was the Sunday after Queen Victoria died, and all the parishioners were in black or mourning dress. During his long service in Fareham, he was always very diligent in his visiting, which he did on a trusty old bicycle to the farthest corners of the parish. A man of boundless energy, in his off-duty moments he was a keen entomologist, and before some readers reach for the dictionary, that means he collected butterflies. James Tarbat left Fareham in 1928, and died nine years later in 1937 at the age of 73. His place at Fareham was taken by the Rev. Alexander Cory, who also gave excellent service to the parishioners for a good number of years.

The vicars at S.S. Peter and Paul had to have a sense of humour, for the choirboys were well known for their little pranks, such as stink bombs, or dead rats left on the pulpit. The Rev. John Ray, who was Curate in the pre-war years, did have a sense of humour. He was also a well known local playwright and music composer, and in 1937 he wrote a special pantomime based on "Dick Whittington" which drew large audiences to every performance. But even some of those buried at this church displayed a sense of humour on occasion, as depicted on the tombstones of a certain Emmanuel Bad, Esquire, in 1632. It contains a lengthly epitaph, but I feel the last two lines may be sufficient, they read:

"So good a Bad doth this same grave contain,
Would all like Bad were that with us remain".

For our next Fareham church we must visit West Street, where the church of Holy Trinity dominates the western end. Holy Trinity Church was built in 1834 to meet the growing needs of the population, and the cost of erection came from funds bequeathed by the will of Lady Thompson, whose son, the Rev. Sir Henry Thompson, was a Curate at S.S.Peter and Paul. A district was assigned to Holy Trinity in 1837.

The church is an early example architecturally of the Gothic revival style, which had come into favour at the beginning of Queen Victoria's reign. A brick edifice with stone dressings, it comprised a small chancel, nave aisles, north and south porches, and a battlemented western tower with spire, added in 1837 and containing a clock and two bells. The church was restored in 1889 at a cost of £510 to provide 700 sittings. The nave was lengthened and a new chancel, organ chamber and vestry were built in 1913, so the building that we see today is vastly different from the original of the last century. The pre-war name that we associate with Holy Trinity is that of the Rev. Andrew Bracken Hargrave, who took over as Vicar in 1923. Mr. Hargrave must be one of the few, perhaps only, members of his calling to have performed the opening ceremony of a cinema. This he did in 1928 when the old Alexandra Cinema in West Street was re-opened after being completely re-constructed.

Whilst Holy Trinity Church still functions in West Street, I am afraid our next church building can no longer be seen, this was the Wesleyan Methodist Church situated opposite Savoy Buildings, more or less facing F.W.Woolworth. This church, which was erected in 1875 at a cost of around £3,000, replaced an earlier structure that had been originally built in 1812. But a few short steps away down West Street there was another church that is no longer on that site, this was the Baptist Church that was originally opened in March, 1899. It was situated between Hartlands Road and the Co-op department store, and disappeared from this location in the 1930s. The Baptists moved to Gosport Road, taking over an old building that had formerly served as a factory for the Portsdown Mineral Water Company. The church building was demolished in the late 70s in the cause of road widening, but has since been replaced by a splendid church in the modern style.

The Congregationalists have a long history in Fareham, in fact it can be traced back to the 1690s. Under the guidance of the first Pastor, the Rev. Samual Chandler, a chapel was erected during that period in West Street. The next landmark for the church came in 1835, when, thanks to the efforts of the Rev. G. Mudie, a new chapel in the Early English style was erected at a cost of £1,350. Despite the many changes that have taken place around it in the past 150 years, this church still adds a touch of peace and tranquility to West Street.

Those of the Catholic faith are catered for in the form of the Sacred Heart Church at the lower end of Hartlands Road, founded in 1873, and rebuilt in 1878. I am not a Roman Catholic, but I must confess that it always gives me pleasure when I am afforded the opportunity to enter this quaint little church, for it harbours an aura of warmth and welcome that many of its bigger brothers decidedly lack.

When studying some of the places of worship that abounded in the area surrounding Fareham, I am afraid that I cannot supress a giggle when I see the descriptions printed in the pre-war Kelly's Directory. It reads as follows: CATISFIELD, a hamlet with a small chapel of ease. CROCKER HILL, a hamlet with a small chapel of ease. FONTLEY, a hamlet with a small chapel of ease. WALLINGTON, a hamlet with a brewery Oh well, you worship who you want to, and the people of Wallington will worship what they want to! Mention of Fontley, or Funtley, whichever you prefer, reminds me of the unique little church there that was built in 1836. It started life as a school, doubling as a place of worship on Sundays, but when a new school was opened in 1880 the old building was used as a church only, mainly by the brickmakers and their families. Along with the brick kilns, the church also provided a means of refuge in which the young men of Fontley might hide from the raiding press gangs from Portsmouth.

For my final place of worship in the Fareham area, I have chosen to return to Peel Common, where in addition to that magnificent windmill there was another unique structure known as the Peel Common Evangelical Church, in fact, this church still flourishes. Let us go back to one quiet Sunday afternoon in May 1900, a small group of people are gathered on the pasture opposite the windmill, and they attract the attention of several local children playing in the area. Before long the sound of a harmonium accompanied by voices singing songs of praise breaks into the still of the countryside.

That joyful group included Samuel Hardiman and his wife Eleanor, their friend Mr. Holgate, and another friend, Miss Longland. That first meeting did not exactly set the world on fire, but on the following Sunday they attracted a few more spectators, not only children, but parents also. This dedicated band were blessed by a fine summer that year, and week by week their numbers began to swell. In that tranquil setting, in the open air with the birds singing and the lush grass under their feet, they must have felt that they were that little bit nearer to the Lord.

Winter arrived, and not wishing to lose any of their flock, Eleanor Hardiman rented the front room of a cottage on the nearby brickfield. With the formation of a Sunday School, it was not long before that room was at bursting point, so in 1902 they were pleased to move into a building constructed of corrugated iron and wood, purchased cheaply from the Rev. Duke-Baker of Botley. It could now truly be called a Mission.

The enthusiastic supporters of the church included Henry Sandford, John Parham, Charles Snook, William Pyle, Colonel Elling, and Alfred Munday. The latter gentleman married Eleanor and Samuel's daughter Mary, and in addition to his lifelong work for this place of worship, Alfred also served on the Fareham Council for many years, and at one time was its Chairman. The Hardimans had their dreams realised in 1926, when after much prayer and self-sacrifice, the money was raised to build a new mission hall. Built by local builders John Hunt, it must have been like the Albert Hall compared to the old tin hut that they had used for 24 years. The Lord had "provided".

Eleanor Hardiman died in 1929, and Samuel followed her in

1936, the mantle of leader fell on to the shoulders of Alfred Munday, and he remained as Pastor until 1966. His wife Mary died in 1972, and Alfred passed away himself in 1976. But the family connection continues, for their son Clifford Munday and his wife Ethel still work hard at furthering the cause of the mission founded by his grandparents, and with the Pastor, Mr. W. Chalmers, they are pleased to welcome worshippers young and old. I cannot get out for Sunday services at Peel Common as much as I would like to, but I can guarantee that whenever I do, my mind always strays back to that scene of over 80 years ago, and the thought of that small band of believers gathered around a harmonium on the common.

That concludes our look at some of the older churches in the Fareham area, and I am pleased to say that several newer places of worship have been added in more recent years. These are built mostly in the modern style, and I cannot refrain from commenting that architecturally some of them remind me more of fire stations than churches, but I suppose we have to move with the times. St. Columbia's Church off Highlands Road, built in the early 60s, is a typical example of a purpose-built church to serve the community that surrounds it. The Church of St. John the Baptist is rather similar, built in the same period, it stands on the corner of Redlands Lane and St. Michaels Grove. But, it does not really matter what a church is like structurally, does it?

Learning the Three 'R's in Fareham.

I have always felt that going to school is like being in the Army, when you are in you wish that you were out, and when you are out you wish that you were back in. I suppose it is the human trait for only remembering the good moments, with events such as receiving six-of-the-best from the headmaster or having to double around the barrack square on the orders of a screaming sergeant-major being cast to the back of the mind, whilst the comradeship of old pals remains with us forever.

Akin to neighbouring Gosport, Fareham has enjoyed the presence of a number of fine old schools through the years, but, unlike Gosport, it has one particular school that has dominated the local education scene for hundreds of years, I refer of course to Price's College. This renowed place of education was founded through the benevolence of Mr. William Price, a Fareham man who was a respected timber merchant in the town. In the terms of his will in 1721 he bequeathed financial support for a school and for the relief of poor widows, the money coming from his estates at Crocker Hill and Elson.

William Price directed that his house in West Street should be utilised for the school, and also to provide living quarters for the master, who was paid a yearly salary of £52. The sum of £60 was allowed for clothing the pupils, who numbered thirty poor children of the parish, comprising both boys and girls at that time. The school in West Street was on the site of what was later to house the fire station, the old station of course, and the pupils could be seen parading outside in their distinctive uniforms made of blue cloth.

The Vicar and Churchwardens of the parish were trustees of the school, so you can be certain that religion played a large part in the curriculum. The entrance exam was run on these lines: they were held every Ash Wednesday and aspiring pupils had to read a passage from the Bible. If pupils were deemed suitable, they were formally accepted and taken away to be measured for one of those famous blue uniforms. During the first half of the last century the old school building was in a sad state of repair, so the trustees decided to rebuild the premises in 1842. It is interesting to note that from this period the school was for boys only, the girls no doubt being sent to the new National School.

Discipline at Price's was tough in those days, and masters were not backward in the use of the cane, even for trivial offences. But this did not stop the "Bluecoat Boys" from getting up to the usual

Old Funtley Church.

Funtley School, 1924.

Baptist Church, Gosport Road, before its demolition, 1979.

Funtley School, 1953.

S.S. Peter and Paul.

Peel Common Evangelical Church.

Trinity Church.

pranks of childhood, and lively moments were experienced in the area of West Street. On Sundays, onlookers may have been excused for thinking how angelic the boys were, for they always assembled at 9-30 in the morning for prayers and instruction at the school, following which they marched in an orderly fashion arm in arm up the High Street to the church on the hill, Bibles and prayer books clutched in their free hands. Once inside the church they had to sit on seats allotted to the school, with Mr. Daniel Wrapson, the master, placed so that he could keep his eagle eye on the lads, and woebetide them if anyone misbehaved. After the service they marched back to the school and broke ranks but not for long, for they had to meet later for evensong, so it was a case of marching back to the church again.

By 1907 the old West Street building was found to be sadly below standard, the outcome being that the Charity Commissioners decided to build a new school, a Board of Governors was formed and the Rev. Tarbat was appointed Chairman. The new school was erected in Park Lane, formerly known as Puxol Lane, and the first headmaster was Mr. S. Bradley. When Mr. Bradley retired in 1934 his position was filled by Mr. George Ashton.

Over the following years, Price's has maintained an excellent reputation, producing many thousands of scholars who have gone out into the world and distinguished themselves in public and military careers. So, the founder of this educational establishment, William Price, would indeed have been proud that his benevolence has been put to such good use and has produced such excellent results.

In the early half of the last century the area of Fareham that includes Park Lane, or Puxol Lane, was rather countrified, in fact there were only two houses in the road we know as Trinity Street. It was here that a school was opened in 1828, and once again it was established thanks to the generosity of the Thompson family. At first it accommodated both boys and girls in one small classroom, but by 1838 it was found necessary to enlarge the building at a cost of £700, and boys and girls were afforded separate classes.

The names that we associate with this school from the last century are that of Joseph Tate and Elizabeth Goodchild, and they were followed in 1860 by Frederick Lowman as headmaster, who was to remain in this position for a remarkable 45 years. Of course, in the old days parents had to pay for their children to go to school, the fee being tuppence a week, later raised to threepence. The general school-leaving age was twelve years, but some left even earlier. It was during the latter part of Mr. Lowman's service that the school was enlarged and modernized, in 1893 to be exact. By this time the area surrounding the building had been developed considerably, and it was officially known as Gordon Road School. A new Senior School was opened in Harrison Road in the 1930s, and the old school in Gordon Road that had given so many years of service, was demolished in 1935.

A small Infants School was erected in 1853 in Western Lane (Osborn Road) at a cost of £400, and was enlarged considerably in 1902 to accommodate 200 children. The names within living memory that we associate with this school are those of Miss Dowling, and later Mrs Linter. The Wickham Road School was built in 1877 and enlarged in 1894; some older readers might remember Miss Kate Windebank who was in charge of the girls, and Miss Hilda Yeates who did her best to control the infants.

I have already mentioned the little mixed school in Fontley that was erected in 1880 at a cost of £1,300, and readers might recall Charles Clark who was headmaster there for many years, but more will remember his successor, Percy Bennett, a "Mr.Chips" if ever there was one. This school also served as a library for Fontley residents; it opened in 1925 on Monday evenings only, and Mr. Bennett was the Librarian. The formidable Percy also operated a private scheme by which you could bring your own books for changing.

By the 1930s a mixed school had been added in Redlands Lane under Miss Hale, a senior boys school in Southampton Road under George Sims, and of course the Harrison Road school for senior girls under Miss Ings.

Name-Dropping.

Most towns and cities take great pride in recording the fact that a famous person was born there, resided there, or perhaps merely passed through the place. In times past the makers of plaques must have enjoyed a very good living, and although this practice has died out to a certain extent, I am pleased to say that there has been a mini-revival in recent times, and quite rightly so, for we should be proud of our heritage.

To my knowledge, the most recent plaque to adorn the fascia of an historic building was erected in Fareham High Street, this was to commemorate Sir John Goss, renowned musician and composer. His father, Joseph Goss, came to Fareham in the late 1700s and served as organist at the parish church. John Goss was born in 1800, and it was to be his destiny to set the music world alight over the following eighty years. He left Fareham to go to the Royal Chapel in 1811, then a few years later he became a pupil of Thomas Attwood, the organist at St. Paul's Cathedral. When Attwood died in 1838, John Goss took over at St. Paul's. His many compositions are far too numerous to list in this humble publication, for he was writing practically right up until his death in 1880. A tablet to his memory was erected in the Crypt of St. Paul's, and now I am pleased to say that we have one in Fareham High Street, at No. 21.

Where the bus station now dominates the corner of West Street and Portland Street, there was once a row of old cottages, one of these was known as Thackeray House, named so because of its association with the renowned novelist, William Makepeace Thackeray. Born in India in 1816, William came to Fareham as a young lad to stay with his great-grandmother after his father died. The town must have provided the young Thackeray with inspiration, for he went on to write himself a permanent place in the Hall of Fame. With this literary connection, it was quite fitting that the old West Street house was used as the Fareham Reading Room and Library in the early 1900s, but I am afraid the demolition hammer struck in the 1920s to make way for the aforementioned bus station.

On the other side of West Street, practically opposite the Thackeray residence, stood a fine old house that had some claim to fame as being the birthplace of Alexander Mackonochie, who became a household word in the last century by indulging in a battle of controversy with the ecclesiastical authorities in London. Alexander was born in Fareham in 1825.

Another famous name that has associations with both Fareham and Gosport is that of Henry Cort, the inventor of malleable iron. Hailing originally from Lancaster, Henry came to this area in 1776 and set up forges at The Green in Gosport and at Fontley in Fareham by the River Meon. He was in partnership with Samuel Jellicoe, and received some financial backing from his father, Adam Jellicoe, a liasion that was to bring Henry Cort's downfall. We have Henry Cort to thank for inventing a process to convert hard pig iron into a soft and useable condition, he also devised a system of making wrought iron into bars by means of grooved rollers.

The results of Cort's inventions had an amazing effect on the iron industry, for it had been dying with only a production of 17,000 tons a year, but following his discoveries production leapt to 250,000 within twenty years. Unfortunately, Adam Jellicoe died owing the Admiralty a considerable sum of money, it held Cort responsible and seized his patents. In many ways it could be said that Henry "was taken to the cleaners" in his financial dealings, for it was estimated that his inventions had added £600 million to the nation's wealth, yet he died in poverty. He was buried in Hampstead Parish Churchyard in Lancashire, and at least they afforded him the honour of providing a bronze tablet in rememberance for his good works. Traces of the iron works at Fontley can still be seen, and followers of industrial architecture visit the site regularly.

I very much doubt if many Fareham people realize that a famous acting family originated from the town, the Melfords. Their story took me some years of research, and I feel that the chief facts are well worth recounting. It began in the middle of the last century with a Fareham tradesman named Jim Smith, a marvellous character who was well known in the town for his wit and satire. You know the type, they stop you in the street and say: "Here, have you heard this one?." Anyway, Mr. Smith had two sons who inherited their father's flamboyant characteristics, and they both had their hearts set on a career in showbiz. But Alfred and Mark Smith realised that their names were not exactly the type to leap out at one from a theatre-bill, so they took the stage-name of Melford.

At a tender age, Mark Melford joined a Portsmouth troupe of actors known as "The Wandering Thespians", who played mainly at the Theatre Royal. He also joined a travelling show at one time, the proprietress of which was a fiery gypsy lady who paid him 15s a week. He certainly had to work for it, for in "Hamlet" he played Horatio, Rosencrantz, and Guildenstern. All in the same performance! In later years he developed a magic act and went on the variety stage as "The Great Rhymeo". He was assisted in the act by his brother Alfred, who by this time was billed as Austin Melford. Although unintentionally so, their act was quite hilarious at times, for they used two white guinea pigs that had a habit of running off during the performance, and the antics of Mark and Austin in trying to recapture the animals had their Portsmouth audiences in stitches.

Mark turned to more serious stuff and began making a name for himself as an actor and playwright, he enjoyed many successes and was still writing up until his death in 1914. That great character actor, Bransby Williams, was a close friend of Mark Melford, and performed a farewell speech at the funeral.

In the meantime, Austin Melford had also been winning acclaim for his acting work, and was established as a firm favourite at the Drury Lane Theatre. A versatile actor, and a master of make up, Austin was still acting shortly before he died in 1908. He had married Alice Batey, and she bore him two sons, both of whom were to become well known in the theatre. The eldest, also named Austin, was actually born in Alverstoke in 1884, and made his first stage appearance at the age of two months on the stage of the Theatre Royal in Portsmouth. He went on to make a good living on the stage and in films, as an actor and director. Austin lived to the ripe old age of 86, his last stage appearance being in "Blue for a Boy" with Fred Emney. His brother, Jack Melford, who was born in 1899, also enjoyed a successful career in entertainment. He made several films, including that old George Formby classic "It's in the Air".

Although Jack died in 1972, it was not the end for the acting Melfords, for his daughter Jill, who was born in 1934, followed the family tradition. Jill Melford has acted in England and America on the stage and in films, notably "The Servant" and "Father Dear Father", and is a regular face on the small screen. She was married to John Standing, actor son of Kay Hammond. So there we are, and to think that it all began in Fareham.

Home Sweet Home.

Throughout its history Fareham has enjoyed the presence of several imposing residences, places that the wealthier members of society have been pleased to call home. And of course, so would the poorer members if they had had the chance! In the following

Blenheim House School, West Street. Near where Dodge City is now sited.

West Street from the corner of Kings Road, 1906.

Fareham actor, Austin Melford, Snr.

Bath Lane in quieter days.

Blackbrook Place.

Portland Street.

Cams Hall, c.1800.

paragraphs I will remind readers of a few of the more resplendent abodes that graced the local landscape.

One of the first known houses in Fareham was Roche Court, situated off the Wickham Road, and built for Peter Des Roches in the 13th Century. Through the ages many alterations were made to the structure of the building, and very little remains of the original. Going back in time to when Fareham was not much more than a village, Roche Court was really out on its own, surrounded by fairly dense forest, rather like the New Forest. From the Des Roches', the house and estates passed through marriage to the Brocas family, beginning in 1381 with Sir Bernard Brocas. The next change came in 1661, when Jane Brocas married Sir William Gardiner; it remained in the hands of the Gardiner family until the death of Sir John Brocas Gardiner in 1868, the baronetcy becoming extinct. In the following years the successors to the property have included Mr. H.F. Rawstorne and Admiral Sir William De Salis, and in the post-war years the premises have been used by the Navy, and as a preparatory school.

Not far from Roche Court, at the top of North Hill stands Uplands House, once the home of the aforementioned Samuel Jellicoe, a former purser in the Royal Navy who had interests in the iron mill works at Fontley. Of course, the Jellicoe family is renowned in the history of naval warfare, Earl Jellicoe carrying on the tradition with great success in the 1914–18 war.

Built at the end of the 18th Century, Uplands had very extensive grounds, in fact Price's School grounds now occupy part of the original estate. The view in the early days must have been magnificent from the house, surrounded by gardens that required seven gardeners to tend them. It also had an artificial lake with an ornamental island in the middle, the whole surrounded by trees.

Following Samuel Jellicoe, the house was in the hands of the Batten family for many years. Around the 1850s a military gentleman in the form of Captain Beardmore lived at Uplands, and he was responsible for amassing a fine collection of arms and armour that was kept in the ballroom. A member of the famous Waterlow family of printers occupied the house after Captain Beardmore, and by the beginning of this century it was lived in by John Norton, a director of the Cunard Shipping Company. During the following years the building underwent several alterations structurally, but houses such as this require an awful lot of money to keep them going, and a veritable army of servants. I am pleased to say that Uplands is still in existence, and gives good service as a home for the elderly.

Sadly, the next Fareham house on our list has not fared as well, for the decaying shell that we know as Cams Hall in the 1980s is far removed from the once resplendent mansion that once graced this site. It would appear that a manor house stood there as far back as the Domesday Survey, with the name varying from Cammes in the 13th century, to Cammes Oysell in the 14th, and Camoyse Orsell in the 16th. General Carnac had a large residence built on the site in the 18th Century, which was taken over by Peter Delme in 1781. The Delme family had bought Place House (Titchfield Abbey) in 1741, and although most ladies would have been more than happy with this palatial residence, I am afraid Peter Delme's wife Betty was decidedly not, for she was a lady with very expensive tastes.

To keep his beautiful wife happy, Peter Delme agreed to move house to the Cams area, and because of its closer proximity to Portsmouth they could accept more readily the invitations to attend the various naval functions of that period. Cams was also a good spot for hunting, shooting, and deer-stalking. They decided to practically rebuild the former residence, and to enlarge it considerably. Now, this was an expensive project, so the Delmes dismantled a good deal of Place House at Titchfield and transferred the materials to Cams for the new building. It did not stop at bricks and stones, for staircases, oak beams and panelling were removed from the medieval palace. Parts were even taken from the Titchfield chapel that Lady Wriothesley had had specially built, and they were used for the construction of stables at Cams Hall. They were probably the most ornate and unique stables in the world, with wonderful carvings from the chapel adorning the surrounds of the horse-boxes.

The by-product from those stables must have proved very useful, for the building was surrounded with masses of flower beds containing a great variety of plants and shrubs. In fact, at one time the grounds kept 25 gardeners fully employed! As one drove up the drive, what a wonderful picture Cams Hall must have made in those days. To the west of the Hall there was an avenue of oak and elm trees known as Bathing House Grove, to the east there was the Cams Plantation, whilst to the south there was a laurel grove and an area called the Wilderness. The view from the terrace was quite magnificent, overlooking the Fareham estuary and providing a grandstand view of the teeming maritime life in Portsmouth Harbour.

With its Ionic columns the main building was impressive by any standards from the exterior, but the interior was just as lavish. One object of decor in the stately long drawing room that was sure to catch the eye of the visitor was a magnificent painting by Sir Joshua Reynolds, showing Lady Betty and her two children. This renowned portrait painter's talents did not come cheaply, yet another example of this lovely lady's extravagance. I suppose her husband should have been grateful that credit cards had not then been invented!

Cams Hall remained in the hands of the Delme family through most of the 19th Century passing to John Delme, henry Delme, and Seymour Delme. I like one story about the Hall that took place in Queen Victoria's reign, it concerns a complaint made by Squire Delme to the Admiralty that he feared that target practice from men-o-war in the harbour would result in damage to his fine property. Following this, a group of merry midshipmen from H.M.S. Excellent planned a jolly jape, they rowed up the creek under the cover of darkness and planted a large cannonball under the drawing room window of Cams Hall. Imagine Squire Delme's face in the morning!

On the death of Sir Seymour Delme, Cams Hall passed out of the hands of the Delme family, and it was sold in 1895 for £10,250. That famous Reynold painting was put up for auction at Christie's and raised 11,000 guineas, then in 1937 it was sold to an American gallery in Washington. Montague Foster was one of the many distinguished owners who had Cams Hall in the following years, and in the Second World War it was used by the Admiralty. As I stated previously, Lady Betty's dreamhouse is now in a very sorry state of dilapidation, although in recent times schemes for restoring the building back to it's former splendour have been proposed, it still remains unrestored. Perhaps one day it will regain its splendour.

Ākin to Uplands, Blackbrook House still serves a useful purpose, it is a maternity home. An attractive Georgian residence on the road to Titchfield, it was built about 1782, following the style of architecture that was popular in England around the time of the French Revolution. It was built in Beaulieu brick, although these soon became covered by creepers, and in addition to the fine views to be seen from the house in those days, it was surrounded by an abundance of fine trees and flower beds. The interior included a magnificent library with a marble mantlepiece, plus twenty bedrooms just in case visitors should decide to pop in unexpectedly. Even so, considerable extensions were added to the building in 1890. The house was occupied for many years by Sir William Biddulph Parker and Lady Kathleen Parker, a gracious couple who were held in high esteem by Fareham residents, lending their spacious grounds for countless charity fetes and suchlike. Their son, Sir William L. Parker, took the property over in later years, he was a much respected local magistrate, and a celebrated horticulturist.

Not too many steps away from Blackbrook House, on the other side of Titchfield Road, stands the beautiful thatched residence known as Bishopswood. It was originally named Blackbrook Grove, but when the house was taken over in 1927 as a residence for the succeeding Bishops of Portsmouth, it was renamed Bishopswood.

Fareham's Historic High Street.

When we think of a High Street, we are usually reminded of a bustling thoroughfare thick with shops and shoppers. In Fareham, West Street is such a street, therefore allowing the town to retain one of the most unique and unspoilt High Streets in Hampshire. With its large number of superb entrance columns and pediments, this street absolutely reeks Georgian elegance. It is not difficult to understand why this area of the town was popular with retired naval officers, for they enjoyed the mild climate and it was still close enough to Portsmouth Harbour to keep in touch with naval events.

Although I have not the space to cover every residence, I will attempt to take readers on a mini-tour of the High Street and point out a few of the places that can still be seen. The street numbers run numerically rather than odds and evens, thus making the task a trifle easier. One of the most attractive qualities of the High Street are the many courts and alleys that lead off it, with inviting arches forming entrances to delightful little mews residences, with beams reminding us of a much gentler Elizabethan age.

I have already mentioned the Victorian lamp-posts that may be seen in the High Street, and other favourite pieces of street furniture are the old insurance plaques that were affixed to the exterior of houses, two fine examples may be seen on the facing walls of No. 11 and No. 16, Norwich and Phoenix companies respectively. Another fact that I recorded earlier was that Lord Lee's mother, Mrs. Melville Lee, lived at No. 12, and this building still displays the outstanding entrance porch that this good lady must have passed through countless times. A few doors away at No. 21 is the house that marks the birthplace of the aforementioned Sir John Goss, complete with commemoration plaque supplied by the Fareham Society. Next door is Lothian House, a fine 18th Century structure.

At one time there was at least two public houses in this area of the High Street, the Coach & Horses and The Golden Lion. The former was demolished around the middle of the last century, but I am pleased to say that the latter is still serving pints for pleasure. Of course, if you do not want the wife to know that you have been drinking when you get home, one way to disguise the tell-tale fumes might be to munch a sweet. It so happens that there was a sweetshop handy just a few doors past The Golden Lion at No. 30a, kept by Mrs Best, or George Bone in earlier days. The name Old Sweetshop Cottage still provides a clue of the former existence of this establishment.

Nearby at No. 34 you would have once heard "Chopsticks" being played on the piano by the pupils of Miss Mabel Rutland, teacher of music, competing with the revving of cars and motorcycles from the neighbouring workshop of Mr. Hansford, a business name that still adorns this end of the High Street. The site was taken over by Mr Hansford in the 1920s, but prior to this it was used as a carriage hire business by Mr. Godwin, and as a dairy by Mr. Holloway.

Church Place is one of my favourite parts of the High Street, the row of charming cottages with a small green in front lead to the peace and tranquility of the churchyard of S.S.Peter and Paul, where several Fareham personalities were laid to rest, names such as Price, Paddon, Coles, Thresher, and Sandy.

Although it is not actually in the High Street, the large building that stands on the corner of Wickham Road must not be neglected, for it is the Old Manor House, now occupied by a firm of solicitors. A fine 18th Century brick building with three storeys, it has a splendid porch with a curved hood and carved Corinthian columns. It was formerly the home of Fareham's Bennett family, Sir William Bennett being appointed High Sheriff of Hampshire in 1761.

Moving back down the High Street, we will find a varied and interesting row of buildings including Vosper House, the Old Vicarage at 46 where Mr. Tarbat resided for so many years, and the impressive stucco facade of the 19th Century building now used by Vosper Thornycroft, formerly the residence of Captain Cunliffe.

Next door to Mr. Collins butchers shop, in the early part of this century there resided one of the town's most outstanding characters, Mrs Grace Russell. This remarkable lady lived to celebrate her 107th birthday, and was well known for her dress-making skills. Fareham resident Mrs Agnes Hunt, who at the age of 92 had particularly fond memories of Mrs Russell, as Miss Merritt, joined the Russell establishment in 1904 as an apprentice dressmaker. She cycled from her home in Wickham to Fareham every day, the working hours then being 8 a.m. to 8 p.m., long hours indeed for a 14 year old girl.

Because of Mrs Russell's advancing years, the dressmaking business was run by one of her daughters, Miss Agnes Russell, a rather strict person to work for. The Russell family, who actually lived at the High Street premises, were very strong Wesleyans. Another daughter, Miss Lizzie Russell, was a big robust lady who did outstanding work as a midwife in Fareham. This reminds me of another lady who was well known for her services as a midwife, Mary Cresswell in Gordon Road; she came to Fareham in 1896 and during the next forty years she delivered over 2,500 babies.

How on earth did I get on to delivering babies, let us get back to the High Street! The ornate Victorian structure that is now numbered No. 63 was lived in for many years by the aforementioned Leonard Warner, a gentleman who had his finger in several Fareham pies. Lysses Path that runs off the High Street nearby, leads down to the creek at Bridgefoot, and in its time was no doubt one of the many avenues used for the once busy trade of smuggling, for this area was honeycombed with courts and passages. In the first half of this century, ground subsidence was a fairly common occurrence in the High Street, with subterranean caverns being discovered at regular intervals under premises there.

The following line of buildings are some of the most impressive in the street, Whittington House at No. 64, Wykeham House School at Nos. 67 and 69, the Fareham & County Club at No. 68, and Kintyre House at No. 70. Whittington House was formerly resided in by Dr. Hugh Case, the Medical Health Officer to the F.U.D.C. The name of Case is well known in the medical history of the town, dating back to 1832 when Dr. William Case commenced practice with Dr. James Ainge. When Ainge retired in 1838, William carried on the practice, assisted in later years by his son George. With his cheery face and fine bedside manner, William Case was a popular figure in the town, and he did excellent work as Fareham's Medical Officer. George Case took over this position when his father died in 1879, thus carrying on the family tradition.

Next to the Georgian elegance of Kintyre House stands its former coach house, a structure that has been tastefully restored in more recent times as a wine bar and restaurant, sporting the name The Old Coach House. I have never been one to let the opportunity for a "plug" to slip by, so I must mention that a few doors away from the coach house the Fareham Book Parlour provides reading matter for everyone, in fact you may have bought this book there, or others in the *Down Memory Lane* series.

Commercial Break over, we now find ourselves in that unique little cut-through known as Union Street, so named because prior to 1836 the Parish Union Workhouse was situated there. In olden days, Union Street was the answer to Southampton's Derby Road, it was a red-light area that abounded in drinking dens and ladies of easy virtue to cater for the needs of visiting sailors. It is difficult to imagine now that this short street once contained two pubs, the Robin Hood and the Blacksmith's Arms, as well as a beerhouse. Therefore it is fairly certain that hardly anyone walked down Union Street, they staggered!

If the area surrounding Church Place is my favourite part to the north of the High Street, then Union Street is certainly my favourite area to the south of it. In fact, one is immediately transformed from the 20th Century into a world that spans several centuries from the moment that one enters Union Street. The outstanding Tudor archway that may be seen from the street is a tourist's dream, and a fine bonus for the artist or photographer. The mention of artists reminds me of a talented lady who still carries out her skills in this quiet little backwater, her name is Marcelle Shears and she is one of the foremost silhouette artists in the country. In her Silhouette Studio she produces life silhouettes that in terms of technique and quality are similar to those that were so popular in the 18th Century, and by using a process of high-lighting that she has developed personally, Marcelle's miniatures have a marvellous three-dimensional effect.

That completes our mini-tour of the High Street area, but the only way that one may fully appreciate the history and architectural splendour of this thoroughfare and its buildings is to visit it personally, for it will be time well spent. Readers may have noticed that I have said little about some of the shops and traders that have flourished in the High Street, this has been reserved for a later section in the book.

Social Services.

I stated a few paragraphs ago that the original Fareham Workhouse was in Union Street, this was in a building that was taken over later for the Robin Hood public house. The Fareham Union Workhouse was erected on the road to Wickham in 1836, the cost being around £5,700. It was intended that this fine brick building should accommodate approximately 300 paupers, but the census of 1841 records that it only had 173 inmates in occupation, and ten years later in 1851 only 169 inmates are listed. Standing on some five acres of land, there was plenty of room for expansion, and a chapel was added in 1849 at a cost of £400.

The Union Workhouse was governed by a Board of Guardians comprising fifteen members, four to represent Fareham, three for Titchfield, two for Wickham, and one each for the other parishes, Portchester, Wymering, Widley, Boarhunt, Southwick, and Rowner. Staff in the early days included Mr. C. Maine as Master, Miss Ann Brock as Matron, John Stedham as Union Clerk, John Wassell and George Ives were the relieving officers, and the Rev. Philip Thresher looked after the spiritual needs of the inmates. In many ways, the old workhouse was like a town on it's own, very self-contained.

If any of the inmates had knowledge of a particular trade, such as boot-mending or cooking, their skills were put to good use and they received extra remuneration for their work. I have a *Hampshire Telegraph* item of 1861 in which the Guardians of the Workhouse state that they wish to interview reliable people for the position of Porter, the person appointed would be provided with board and lodging with washing, the salary being 15/– per annum! But of course, as in most jobs, there were some perks available, for they could earn an extra 6/– per year for haircutting and shaving the inmates!

 FAREHAM'S HISTORIC HIGH STREET

Knowle Hospital, 1916.

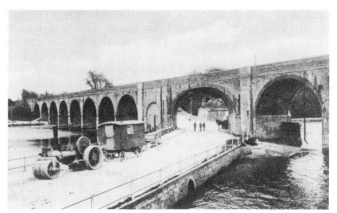

Bridge over bridge, over the creek.

Knowle nursing staff.

Fareham Millpond, before the traffic invasion.

The old workhouse building is still in service on the Wickham Road as St. Christopher's Hospital, and this raises a rather delicate issue, for Fareham residents have been calling for many years for a hospital that is adequate for the vastly-increased population of the town in the 1980s. Newer residents of Fareham will be surprised to learn that there was an isolation hospital in Highlands Road run by the F.U.D.C, it was built in 1887 originally, but was enlarged in 1901 to accommodate 22 patients. There was also a nurses house erected in Southampton Road in 1912, in memory of King Edward VII.

Of course, there is still one outstanding hospital in the Fareham area, the mental hospital at Knowle. We are more sensitive to disorders of this nature now, but in the last century the authorities were more brash and referred to it as the Hants County Lunatic Asylum. This is another establishment that could rate the status of a small town or village, for it covers a large area. It was built in 1852 for the reception of pauper lunatics, the building costing some £15,000, which was exclusive of the £50,000 paid for the purchase of Knowle Farm, which comprised 114 acres. The Asylum usually catered for about 450 inmates in its early days, although it was capable of holding 560. The inmates came from all over Hampshire, and the sexes appeared to be split in number fairly evenly, with the females employed in various domestic duties and the males kept busy in cultivating the farm and gardens.

It was not all gloom and despair for the inmates of Knowle, for even as early as the 1860s events were organized for their pleasure, including dances every two weeks in which patients of both sexes enjoyed themselves singing and dancing for a few hours. Over the years the hospital has been enlarged considerably, including the erection of a small church. The White's Directory of 1859 goes to great lengths to point out that although patients are sometimes held in solitary confinement for short periods, the practice of mechanical restraint is never used. It also adds that the wards are very spacious and well ventilated, and that every effort is made to provide for the comfort and health of the patients. Visitors were also well received, and in later years the hospital had a railway stop on the Meon Valley Line for their convenience.

Mention of this revered railway line, reminds us that it has played a varied role in the history of Knowle Hospital, for in more recent years it was discovered that wayward inmates have actually hidden and lived in the tunnel there for some time. I like the story of an incident that happened in 1935, this was when a porter stationed at Droxford Station noticed a man wandering down the line in the early hours of the morning. He was carrying a water-bottle, and when questioned by the porter he explained that he was carrying his water supply for the day. He went on to say that he had just come from Knowle, and that he could not stay there another moment, for the place was full of Italians. In fact, he was on his way to London to see the Prince of Wales and tell him about all the foreigners in Knowle! The porter, Mr. McRill, gave the man a seat and a cigarette, then phoned for the police. Police Sergeant McNally and Constable Southey duly arrived and escorted the poor chap back to the hospital.

Still on medical matters, I must mention the work of the St. John Ambulance in Fareham. It all began in 1912 when a few enthusiastic first-aiders got together to form a Division, with Mr. Dodge being appointed as Superintendent, and Mr. Chase acting as Secretary. Mr. Knight, who had formerly been a sergeant in the 6th Hants Regiment, was elected Sergeant of the Division, and drills were carried out in strict style at the rear of Mr. Dodge's shop in West Street. A stretcher store was made over the entrance of their headquarters, thus ensuring that a stretcher was always available in case of emergencies.

This eager little band met week after week, and they were so keen that they were selected as a team to represent the area in

1912 at Southampton, to compete for the coveted Twiss Rose Bowl. To their credit they gained second place, which no doubt made Sergeant Knight a very proud man. When the Great War arrived many of the St. John members were called away on active service, but those left behind helped to run Hawkstone, the hospital in Osborn Road. Sadly, after the war the interest began to flag, and the group eventually disbanded. Then, in 1936, thanks to the efforts of Fire Chief Arthur Sutton the Division was reformed with the help of Surgeon Capt. Baxter. Some of the old members became interested again, and by 1937 they were back to full strength. Which was just as well, for another war was just around the corner.

I will bring this section to a close by reminding readers of another noble Fareham institution, the St. Edith's Home at Wallington. Founded by Lady Larcom in 1869, it was primarily for girls between the ages of 14 and 16, and trained them as domestic servants, with an emphasis on cooking and laundry work. In 1884 the home was taken over by the Church of England Society for Waifs and Strays, and it was enlarged and virtually rebuilt in 1907. This building may still be seen, for as the Roundabout Hotel it is passed every day by thousands of motorists.

On The Waterfront.

A directory of 1847 informs readers that: "The principal source of prosperity for Fareham is to be found in the water communications that it enjoys." We must remember that this was written after the railway had arrived in the town, a form of transport that tended to reduce the work of town quays, But, it is true, Fareham Quay was a hive of industry in the middle of the last century, with ships flying the flags of Germany, France, Russia, and Denmark visiting Fareham with merchandise. In turn they loaded exports such as timber, bark, hoops, pottery, bricks, whiting for making clay pipes, and chalk from the Wallington pits. The chalk was mostly shipped to the Isle of Wight for the cement-making industry, with cargoes sailing from Sutton's Quay near the old mill at Cams. Most of the chalk was taken from John Holt's chalk pit at Boarhunt, a lime making industry being carried on there at one time. There was also a chalk pit at Dow Paddock, later Main Dell, on the site of the Fareham waterworks.

There was also a brisk coal trade from the quay, with families driving in from Fareham's outlying villages in order to collect coal. Some of them would start the journey from their homes at midnight, and perhaps not arrive home until the middle of the following day.

Troops embarked from Fareham Quay for the Peninsular Wars in locally-built ships, and during the Napoleonic struggles there were a number of huge grain stores around the quayside that were converted into sick bays for the wounded. A large number of military men died here and were buried in Fareham, the site of the gravestones was called Hospital Yard. There was also a hospital field near the quay where many French prisoners-of-war were brought to their last resting place from Portchester Castle.

In 1807 there was quite an impressive scene enacted at Fareham Quay, this was when the Water Bounds were traced between Fareham and Portsmouth. The *Hampshire Telegraph* describes the scene most vividly. The Fareham folk would not let the Pompey officials land, so Mr. Goodson the Portsmouth Mayor caught two Fareham lads and flogged them in a boat at the side of the quay. The Fareham residents caught two Portsea boys and rendered the same treatment. Ouch! And this was all supposed to be in fun! Anyhow, after these jollifications both parties adjourned to the frigate *Laurel* for a grand bunfight. During the dinner, the Mayor of Portsmouth observed that the Town Clerk, Mr. Calloway, was rather the worse for drink, and said: "Sir, you are tipsy, dead drunk." To which Mr. Calloway replied: "Drunk perhaps, but dead, not yet sir!" Hic!

I mentioned smuggling in the earlier section on the High Street, and no story relating to Fareham Quay and Creek would be complete without a few words on this illicit trade. I have an account of a story that was related by resident George Towell in the 1930s, this concerned his father, who as a ten year-old lad in 1836 witnessed an incredible scene near the waterfront. A small vessel slipped into Fareham waters one evening, somehow escaping the attention of the Fareham Customs Official. It was thought that the official was decoyed by means of a hoax message. Anyhow, it became obvious that the craft had a cargo on which the shipper did not intend to pay duty. It was also apparent that the shipment was expected, for on arrival at the Quay it was unloaded in double-quick time!

The last wagon left the scene in the early hours of the morning, drawn by three horses. As it rumbled up Quay Lane (Street), the wagon was met by an official of the law. His order to stop was ignored, so he drew a pistol and promptly shot down one of the horses. The smugglers retaliated by dealing the same fatal treatment to the official's steed, and the horse fell on to its rider to render him unconscious. The smugglers hastened and heaving the dead horse aside, they harnessed the remaining two horses and disappeared into the distance like Ben Hur on his chariot!

Meanwhile, the vessel at the quay had cast off, and as it had no contraband on board, it escaped as free as a whistle. Of course, the incident may have been seen by a few of the local residents who habitually haunted the quayside, but silence was assured by the passing of a bottle of spirits or package of tobacco. Smuggling operations such as this probably accounted for many of the ghost stories that abounded around that time, with spectral horses and riders reported hurtling through the streets of Fareham in the dead of night!

Striking a more cheerful note, the quay was the scene for much fun and gaiety in the last century and the early part of this, I have already mentioned the marvellous regattas that became part of Fareham's life, although these were sometimes tinged with sorrow, for large crowds gathered around the quayside, and it was a regular occurrence for folk to fall into the creek, sometimes proving fatal. In the 1800s residents called for a fence or railing to be erected by the water's edge. Around this time, Fareham was beginning to enjoy some reputation as a watering spa, in fact, a bathing-house was erected by the creek in 1838 at a cost of £600. As mixed bathing was frowned on, there were separate baths for men and women, both supplied with water at high tide from the creek. This accounts for Bath Lane acquiring its name, for in earlier times it was known as Park Lane, and as I have mentioned earlier, the Park Lane we know today was formerly Puxol Lane. Confusing, is it not?

Over the years, the quay at Fareham has been able to boast a number of colourful characters, one of whom was George Wassell. George was a local boatman, and although he was known by most folk as "Fiery Wassell", he had a soft spot for kids, and would row them across the creek so that they could swim on the Cams side. The son of Joseph Wassell, a well known Fareham river pilot, George lived in Quay Street for over fifty years. Sadly, he was deaf, this followed an accident he had when he fell down the hold of a ship on the quay. George hired out boats for fishing and pleasure, and could be seen at all the big regattas. It was a sad day for Fareham when George Wassell died in 1925 at the age 78.

For Whom The Gate Tolls.

Quite recently I was on a coach travelling across France, and I must admit to becoming increasingly frustrated with the number of

44

road toll barriers that we had to pass through, at the end of the trip I had firmly decided that I would rather pay my road charges the British way, by yearly road tax. With this in mind, think how frustrating it must have been for the old horse-drawn coaches of centuries past, for tollgates were plentiful in and around the Fareham area.

In 1835 there were 36 turnpike roads in Hampshire, their total length amounted to 810 miles, and the income that they brought in annually was approximately £30,000. It is to be hoped that the proprietors enjoyed the money while they had it, for within ten years road traffic was reduced considerably by the expansion of the railway system.

Fareham's busiest turnpike was undoubtedly to the north of the town at the top of North Hill, this being when it was on the main route to the south. There was little chance of coaches crashing through the gate, for by the time the horses had pulled their load up the steep incline of North Hill, they must have been exhausted. During wintery conditions it was quite a common occurrence for the passengers to have to get out of the coach in order to lighten the horses burden when negotiating this hill.

There was a toll cottage to go with the tollgate and tollbar, and one of the last tollkeepers to reside there was a gentleman named William Trodd, one of Fareham's most colourful characters. William never hurried, even when the horses were snorting and stamping the ground by the gate, or the posthorn was being blasted until the blower's teeth were almost falling out, he would not be hurried! He would amble out of his cottage to arrange the toll and subsequently open the barrier, and all the time he would be singing at the top of his voice. William had a brother, Thomas Trodd, living with him at the toll cottage, and Tom was one of the official tailors for Price's School. This was of course when the school was situated in West Street. I mentioned that there was also a tollbar at the top of North Hill, this was installed across the entry

to the highway we know as Kiln Road. The bar had plenty of customers, not only for folk coming to or from Fontley, but also for prospective patients or visitors travelling to Knowle Hospital.

After the new road to Fareham was opened in 1872, the toll business was transferred to the lower end of Old Turnpike, only in those days it was not known as Old Turnpike, it was called North Road. The new tollhouse and gate was sited where the Turnpike Garage is now, and it was looked after by the Matthews family. They really had an eye to business, and could perhaps be credited with starting the first motorway cafe, for before they attempted to open the gate they would insist on selling refreshments to the hungry travellers. As we all know, boys will be boys, and one of the great pranks for local lads during the hours of darkness was to tie a rope on to an old wheelbarrow and drag it past the tollhouse. On hearing the sound of wheels on the roadway, Mr. Matthews would emerge grumbling from his abode, jangling his keys, and giving a cry of "Whoa there". To his amazement, there was not a coach or wagon in sight! This is probably another reason how stories of invisible horsemen were derived!

Some travellers were very devious, and they would try all sorts of tricks to avoid paying toll money. One of their favourite ploys was to enter the town via Pook Lane, Spurlings, and Wallington. The crafty lot!

Before we leave this area of Old Turnpike, I would remind readers of the interesting little almshouses nearby, they were erected in 1850 by Joseph Paddon for two almspeople in memory of his deceased wife.

Making Tracks For Fareham.

It began as a pleasant sort of a day, the sun was shining and all seemed well with the world. Three small toddlers were happily playing in the Recreation Ground at Fareham, as befits the sweet innocence of childhood. Suddenly, one of the kiddies began to

Railway viaduct, Wallington, 1869.

Fareham Creek, 1930s. Mill in background.

Fareham Turnpike.

Fareham Quay in horse-drawn days.

An exceptionally high tide.

climb the nearby railway embankment, and of course, like sheep the others soon followed. Chuckling with delight at this new adventure, they crawled through a gap in the fence at the top of the slope.

They were fascinated with the long metal tracks, not knowing in their innocence that they were railway lines. They were standing over the arches at the bottom of Quay Street, which was close to where the trio lived, when a train appeared as if out of nowhere. The three youngsters, two aged two, and one aged three, were mowed down by the great iron monster in a matter of seconds.

What a tragedy. The whole of Fareham was stunned by the accident, and many folk wept unashamedly when they heard the terrible news. An investigation was called immediately, following which the Southern Railway improved all fences adjoining railway lines, but of course, no measures taken could console the grieving parents of the children.

That sad incident happened in 1928, and it is just one of the many stories that feature in the history of railways in Fareham, I am pleased to say that most of the others strike a much happier note.

Compared with the railway station in neighbouring Gosport, Fareham Station was certainly the poor relation, for the resplendent William Tite designed Gosport Station cost something in the region of £11,000 to erect, whilst Thomas Brassey built the station at Fareham for around £1,400. The line was plagued with trouble in its early days, mainly due to the infamous Fareham Tunnel to the north of the station. Passenger traffic began running on the line to Gosport in November 1841, but after a few days trial the engineer in charge, Mr. Joseph Locke, advised suspension of the service, being fearful about the stability of Fareham Tunnel. This section was prone to land-slips, so Locke and his loyal workmen toiled day and night to overcome the problem and get the line running again as quickly as possible. They eventually won the battle, and the line was opened permanently on 7 February, 1842, but their bad fortune had cost some £15,000 more than the original estimate.

And so, those wonderful smoke-belching monsters became a familiar sight on the local landscape, rumbling over the iron bridge adjacent to the station at Fareham. Try to imagine what it was like travelling by rail in those times, thrilling it surely was, but comfortable it certainly was not. Carriages were constructed more on the lines of the old stage coaches, and unfortunately they were by no means robust enough for rail work, but matters improved when Mr. Joseph Beattie took over the carriage construction depot of the London & South Western Railway Company, with stronger springing being added. First-Class passengers had the bonus of having windows and a roof over their heads, but Second-Class did not have windows, and even worse, Third-Class carriages had neither windows or roof! That was the bad news for Third-Class passengers, the good news being that nobody complained about fellow travellers smoking cigarettes! That is if they could keep them alight, or even on their lips!

Whilst Gosport Station is associated with visits from Queen Victoria, en-route for her beloved Osborne, Fareham had to be content mainly with watching Royalty pass through the station. Although, in the May of 1859 a Royal visitor did alight at Fareham Station. This was Prince Edward of Saxe Coburg Gotha, who was on a visit to inspect the forts and fortifications that were being constructed at Rowner and Frater. This must have been a proud moment for Michael Walsh, for he was the Fareham stationmaster at that time.

Leaping on another twenty years or so, Mr. Watts was the stationmaster when a very merry event took place at the station. This happened in 1880 when James Burley took over the nearby Railway Hotel, and wishing to start off on the right foot, he invited the Fareham railway staff to a special slap-up dinner. Toast followed toast, drink followed drink, and it was not too long before the chaps began to slide slowly under the table. Stoned out of their minds! One may imagine that the following day any passengers alighting at Fareham Station had difficulty in getting anyone to carry their luggage!

Around that time, William Buckmaster was a junior clerk at the station, for he had joined the railway company originally in 1875. For William it was a case of local lad makes good, for he continued to become Assistant General Manager at the Waterloo Station head-office. He was a loyal servant to the L. & S.W.R., for when he started work for them he was only 11 years and eight months old. Incidentally, his father was James Buckmaster, who was clerk to Holy Trinity parish for 58 years.

1903 will go down as the year that the Wright Brothers took to the air, and whilst most of Britain was singing the new song "Down At The Old Bull And Bush", the good people of Fareham were singing the praises of the Meon Valley Railway Line. Many readers will have happy memories of this pleasant little line that ran from Fareham to Alton, stopping along the way at picturesque country stations such as Wickham, Droxford, Warnford, Privett, East Tisted, and Farringdon. For rail enthusiasts it was indeed a sad day when this line closed in February 1955.

A few years after the opening of the Meon Valley line, Fareham Station suffered a spate of baby deaths. In the April of 1907, 11 year old William Brown was playing near the station when he found a brown paper parcel on the entrance path from Titchfield Road, and on closer inspection he saw a child's toe sticking out the edge. Sergeant Day was summoned to the station, and on unwrapping the gruesome parcel he found the body of a newly born baby, a little girl. Well, that was bad enough, but only a week later there was another baby mystery at the station. Sidney Parsons was on duty at the east signal box when he heard a baby crying, and on investigation he found an infant's body lying across the track,

evidently dropped from a passing train. By some miracle, the baby survived the drop with only a slight head graze! This was a baby story for which I can provide an ending, for the police traced the mother and made an arrest. It turned out that she had been prompted into taking this terrible action because she had recently learnt that her soldier husband was returning home that week after service abroad. The baby was a few weeks old, the husband had been away for several years, need I say more!

In 1929, the quick action of station porter Alf Swatton from Paxton Road saved a passenger's life. He was on duty when he saw a lady attempting to get off a moving train, when suddenly she slipped between the footboard and the platform. Young Alf did his Douglas Fairbanks bit and jumped aboard to hold the lady until the train had come to a standstill. My Hero! On the recommendation of Stationmaster Stretch, Alf was presented with a silver watch by the railway company. I recently had the pleasure of meeting Alf Swatton and reminding him about this incident, and I am pleased to say that he still has the presentation watch. Alf made the railway his career, and he was very fond memories of the Meon Valley line, serving at several signal boxes along the way. He retired in 1974, a job well done.

The staff at Fareham Station were renowned for their helpfulness to passengers, especially the ticket collectors. This was a position that was held by George Pratt from the turn of the century for many years, and another popular collector who followed him was Ernie Giles. William Ward was another faithful railways servant, for he worked as a signalman at Fareham for 43 years, until his retirement in 1935. Away from the railway lines he was a local Justice of the Peace.

Readers who are old enough to recall those golden days of the steam engine, will also recollect that it was a common occurrence for passengers to disappear in a cloud of thick smoke, especially when going through a tunnel. With this in mind, think of old Jim

Station Approach, 1906.

Fareham Station.

Glorious days of steam.

Railway bridge from the west.

Tram negotiating a countrified Hoeford.

Tram passing the Rising Sun.

No. 3 turning into Portland Street.

A tram-lined Gosport Road.

Smith, whose favourite occupation was to clamber over the top of Fareham Tunnel. What on earth was he doing up there, I hear you cry! Would you believe that he was catching adders! Jim, who lived in Wallington, did this for a living, for there was a great demand from London hospitals for adders' fat, and they realized 5/- per oz. So Jim, who was surely Fareham's answer to the New Forest's Brusher Mills, took his forked stick to Fareham Tunnel, and could catch as many as forty in one morning. It did not do Jim any harm, for he died in 1933 at the age of 80. Snakes Alive!

Fareham station building has undergone many alterations through the years, a fact confirmed by changes in brickwork and construction from the exterior. But I am pleased to say, despite being the poor relation at birth, the station and railway at Fareham is still flourishing, whilst the once resplendent but now decaying station at Gosport ceased rail operations several years ago. Readers interested in this station are referred to *Transports of Delight* the story of transport in Gosport.

Although one may still savour the delight of rail travel in Fareham, sadly our next form of transport has not been around for over fifty years. Yes, the dear old tramcar. I have covered the local history of the Gosport & Fareham Tramways to some depth in another book in the **Down Memory Lane** series, *Transports of Delight*, so I will provide readers with but a brief reminder of this revered link between the two towns.

Unlike Gosport, Fareham did not have a horse-drawn tram service, but when this system was electrified in 1906 the line was extended to Fareham, terminating at the railway station. It was hoped at one stage to extend the line eastwards from Fareham to Cosham, linking up with the Portsdown and Horndean Light Railway, but unfortunately this never materialized. The Fareham route to Gosport was officially opened for passenger use in January 1906, the fare to Gosport Hard being 4d., or a day return ticket could be bought for 6d. The service ran every 15 minutes.

A power station was built to generate the electrical supply required for running the tramways, this being sited at Hoeford near the Fareham-Gosport boundary line. I expect there are still quite a number of people who can remember the great 160ft. high chimney that went with the power station, for it was not demolished until June 1940.

On some cold winter mornings the trams emerging from the Hoeford Depot had some difficulty in starting through frost and ice on the overhead lines, but they managed to get over this by having a shedhand standing on the top deck with a long yard broom which he ran along the line until the tram could build up speed. The old trams also had cow-catchers on the front like the trains of the Wild West in America, these proved very handy for scooping-up the stray sheep that regularly strayed across West Street.

One of my favourite tram stories concerns tramdriver Ted Cook, one morning early he drove out of the depot and headed for Fareham. A few yards out he came alongside Jack White, a popular travelling fishmonger in the town. One thing led to another, and Jack challenged Ted with his tram to a race against his own donkey and cart. Off they went, you should have seen that donkey go, it was more like Red Rum! The amazing thing is that Jack did not whip the donkey once, he merely dangled a stick against the cart-wheels to produce a rat-tatting sort of a noise. Needless to say, they beat Ted's tram!

Tramdrivers, both men and ladies, had to be very careful when approaching the end of the line at Fareham Station that they did not run off the tracks, for it was quite a performance to get the tram back on. This was usually accomplished by levering it back into position by means of a tow-bar, which was easy enough if you had completed Lesson Six of your Charles Atlas Course!

The section of the line between Brockhurst and Newgate Lane was most pleasant indeed, covering about three miles of open countryside, with just the odd farm cottage here or there. But, it all came to an end in 1929, for 31 December the last tram rumbled into Hoeford Depot, so ending another era in transport history.

So, Fareham entered 1930 with a tramless town, but it did not take the residents long to get accustomed to the motor buses that inherited the roads. The area was served by a varied selection of private bus companies, but over the following twenty years or so they were gradually absorbed by the large operators, Provincial, Hants & Dorset, and Southdown. It was sad to see old established private bus companies such as Tutt's Enterprise fleet disappear from our roads, for the drivers and their vehicles were quite unique, and if you wanted to stop one all you had to do was wave a hand or shake a leg, they would be sure to stop. Try this now!

I should think that as far as Fareham is concerned the most fondly remembered private bus operator was Smith Brothers, a family transport concern that ran a service between Fareham, Fontley, and Knowle Hospital. The travelling public much appreciated the Smith Brothers service, for they provided a valued link for Fontley villagers, patients and visitors to and from the hospital, so it is not surprising that they flourished for almost thirty years until the mid 50s, the route then being taken over by Provincial.

As I have pointed out many times in the past, transport in a way has been a case of dog eat dog, with the railways eating the horse coaches, then in turn being eaten to some degree by electric trams, which were eventually swallowed by the motor bus. The story does not end there, for buses have been severely hit by the rising popularity of the family motor car. Just imagine the excitement of seeing the first horseless carriage arrive in Fareham in the early years of the century, eighty years on the fascination has decidedly cooled, especially when one considers the endless traffic jams that have plagued Fareham for the past twenty years.

In the 20s and 30s, Fareham motorists may have had more room on the roads, but the vehicle speeds were very restricted. This resulted in many battles with the "Boys in Blue", in fact many Fareham drivers were caught in speed traps and subsequently fined for going over 20 m.p.h.! The motorists were up in arms in 1925, many of them complaining that the police speed traps were an underhand way of obtaining extra tax revenue. One well known Fareham resident went as far as to state that he thought grown men might find something better to do than hide behind hedges all day waiting for motorists to drive past! Strong stuff indeed!

Man The Pumps.

I have previously mentioned Arthur Sutton in connection with a section that included the good work of the St. John Ambulance in Fareham, but this was only a small portion of the service that this remarkable man rendered for the town, for he gave fifty years of his life in the cause of firefighting. But, let us go back to the beginning, back to the middle of the last century, when it was still very much a case of "Pass the bucket Fred", whenever a fire should erupt. With the large number of houses built of wood, all that one could really do was stand clear and watch the flames doing their worst.

Influenced by the insurance companies, improved methods of firefighting began to evolve gradually, and in the 1860s even Fareham could boast a form of fire station. Situated in the High Street, it came under the jurisdiction of the Local Board of Heath, which allocated five members to look after the fire department, they were James James, William Sprent, William Case, Richard Porter, and James Blackman. The engineer and surveyor for the Board was John Rosevear, and he was appointed as Superintendent of the Fire Engine House.

Whenever a fire broke out, most of the responsibility fell on the

Fareham Fire Brigade, 1911.

All-England winners, 1913.

Fireman Charles Frost, 1895.

Fareham brigade at drill in Bath Lane, 1910.

shoulders of three men, the engineman, the turncock, and the fire engine manager. On the alarm being raised the manager would get a message to the turncock as quickly as possible, then this chap would turn off the sluices, except those in the main pipe leading directly to the scene of the fire. The idea being to keep the whole pressure of water concentrated to one spot. It was also the turncock's duty to keep the hydrants and sluice valves well oiled and maintained, and to regularly clean and clear the gulley traps. This is how Fareham's fire department proceeded for the following twenty years or so, and it may be said that the only people who were happy with the inefficiency of the fire service were a few farmers. Let me explain, the name of the game was insurance, and if a farmer was having a particularly bad year, it was a fairly common practice to have a fire arranged! With the farms being generally situated out of town, the poor old fire department usually arrived in time to clear up the ashes!

The big breakthrough came in 1888, when the Fareham Fire Brigade proper was formed, with the station being moved to Quay Street, Arthur Sutton, who was a member of the well known family printing business in West Street, joined the brigade on the 20th November, 1888, and was promoted to the rank of Chief Officer by 1894, this being the year that the Urban District Council took over the town's affairs. In those early days of the Fareham Fire Brigade, their equipment included a manual fire-engine, 40 feet of leather hose, and a portable fire escape. The escape was rather bulky, and took seven men to move it. It was fitted with a canvas chute, by which means anyone trapped in a fire could hopefully slide to safety, but during one fire a member of the brigade got his helmet caught at the top of the chute and remained there helplessly suspended, and some anxious moments passed before his comrades could get him free.

George Rand was a very useful member of the Fareham brigade, for he was a sailmaker in the town for over forty years, so they got George to make a water tank of canvas and iron for transporting water to fires where there was not any available. He was also responsible for constructing a canvas jumping sheet, readers will be familiar with this piece of equipment, for it is usually seen in films being held by a circle of chaps, yelling at a poor unfortunate trapped on the window ledge of the top floor of a sky-scraper building to "Jump"!

It was a proud day for Fareham when the brigade took possession of its first horse-drawn steam engine, and large crowds gathered around Holy Trinity Church in West Street to witness the engine's first trial run, the idea being to test the height of the water jet upon the spire of the church. The local fire heroes were doing their stuff when suddenly, the hose burst under pressure and water was sprayed anywhere but where it was intended to spray. Needless to say, onlookers got soaked to the skin!

I think it would be true to say that some of the drills carried out in the early days of the brigade were more reminiscent of the Keystone Cops, or perhaps I should say Quaystone Cops. During one drill on the ground near Bath Lane, Fire Chief Sutton was organizing his men for what was supposed to be a highly efficient operation. The intention was that when Arthur gave a blast on his trusty whistle, the chaps would be galvanized into action. They were just getting themselves sorted out for the operation, when suddenly there was a loud whistle blast, immediately throwing them into confusion and resulting in bodies running here, there, and everywhere. In fact, it was absolute chaos, with firemen bumping into each other right, left, and centre! Arthur Sutton was not a happy man, and directed his gaze towards a clump of bushes, just in time to see a young lad running away with a whistle in his hand. The firemen gave chase, and in his panic the boy ran blindly into the creek with a great splash. The ironic thing was that this affair ended with the firemen having to rescue the lad, for he was stuck fast in the mud and rising tide!

At times of fire it was vital that the horses were harnessed to the appliance in quick time, and this called for a great deal of skill from the chap carrying out the operation. The horses were very often hired from carriers such as Fred Dyke, and of course they played an essential role in the fire team. It was a serious business, the firemen had to meet for fire drill twice a month, and any member not turning up for a fire or two drills in succession had to supply a very good reason. It was also a sin to use bad language or perform practical jokes, and any member found doing so was liable to a fine of five shillings. The standard firemen's kit comprised helmet, cap, an undress and a full dress uniform, boots, spanner, lifeline, and of course a fireman's best friend, an axe.

By 1910 the Fareham Fire Station had moved to West Street, and into that resplendent old building that has been such a familiar sight in the street for many years. The move proved to be a good omen for the Fareham brigade, for with the aid of better equipment and facilities, they went to Birmingham in 1913 and won the All-England Brigade Championships, so just imagine how proud Chief Sutton was when they brought the shield home to Fareham. Their success was partly due to Fireman Wilf Pipe, who outshone the other brigades with his strength and skill at carrying a man down a ladder. So Wilf was given the honour of driving Fareham's first motor fire engine when they took delivery of it.

Charlie Frost was Wilf Pipe's father-in-law, and he was a member of the brigade from the 1880s, and I believe that there was another member of the Frost family in the unit whose name was Jack. Jack Frost? Other members included Mr. H. Clark, who was the Second Officer, two engineers in the form of Henry Fry and Ernie Holdaway, and Mr. Hoare, who was sub-engineer. And of course, leading them through thick and thin there was dear old Arthur Sutton, who retired in 1938 having completed his fifty years. Perhaps this was just as well, for within a year the firefigh-

ters of Fareham and Gosport certainly had their hands full in the area, dealing with enemy bombing.

The Fareham of the 1980s has a fine modern fire station situated near the railway station, equipped with some of the best apparatus available. Well, whatever they have, it just has to be better than a manual fire-engine, 40 feet of leather hose, and a canvas fire-escape!

Leisure And Pleasure.

Although working hours were longer in the old days, it was not always a case of having to slog from morning to night, and if the residents of Fareham had a chance to possibly enjoy themselves, they jolly well took it. It is true that their pleasures were much simpler then, but in many ways I think that they probably enjoyed themselves even more in off-duty pleasure hours than we do today, for one can have too much of a good thing.

I have already mentioned the fairs and circuses that were held in earlier times, and the colourful sailing regattas that once graced the creek, but I would like to devote a few paragraphs to some of the other leisure and pleasure pursuits of bygone years.

Sport is always a good way of working off any surplus energy, and football probably rates as one of the most energetic. Like neighbouring Gosport, over the years Fareham has produced some jolly fine teams. Soccer was very little known in the area until the 1880s, with most of the early teams evolving from schools and churches. Games were generally played in what may be described as a gentlemanly fashion, although there was the odd exception to this rule, for even then they had "dirty" players. Included in this number was a chap named Smyth, who was in fact a master at Foster's School in Stubbington, he really was a hard man to come up against on the football field, and always played a very robust game.

Many young men worked in shops in those days, and the only

Fareham Wednesday F.C., 1924.

Bird in Hand outing, Fanny White extreme right.

1937 Coronation Carnival – Queen Vera Roffey.

Peel Common Church outing.

Fareham Volunteer Territorial cyclists, 1916.

free time that they got off in the week was on Wednesday afternoons. Because of this, Wednesday leagues were formed, and Fareham Wednesday were a team that had their fair share of success in the 20s and 30s. My 1924 photograph of Fareham Wednesday Athletic F.C. will, I am sure, evoke many fond memories, for that was a particularly good year for them. A couple of seasons later they received a sad blow, for one of their star players, Theodore Moxham, died from the results of a local game. Theodore leapt up to head a ball, catching it on his forehead. The ball was extra heavy with mud, and by the end of the match his head was aching badly. The pains got worse over the next two days and in the end Theodore had to go to hospital, where he died shortly afterwards. So 1926 was a season that Fareham Wednesday preferred to forget.

In 1933 it was announced that the financial affairs of Fareham Football Club were in a very criticial state, and fifty years on their position is very much the same, with many supporters fearful that the club may have to close. This would indeed be a very sorry happening, and a terrible blow to the town, so let us hope that the club survives this crisis.

Turning to the calmer sport of cricket, I am pleased to say that Fareham Cricket Club has a fine record, in fact in recent years they celebrated their centenary. During this period, the club has produced a number of fine teams, their halcyon years proving to be the 1950s. It all began in 1882 when the Rev. F.J. Ashmall, a curate at the parish church, decided to form a local cricket club, and within a short time they had a team that was respected far and wide. Their early matches were played on a strip of land at the rear of Trinity Church, but during the first few years of this century they moved to the cricket ground that we still associate the club with, the Bath Lane recreation ground that commands such a pleasant position by the side of the creek.

Mention of the creek reminds us of the formidable role that Fareham's waterfront has played in the pursuit of pleasure, and the influence that Fareham Sailing Club have provided over the years. Whenever I have been away from the area, perhaps on a trip to London, I must admit that it always gives me great pleasure to reach Fareham Quay, for when I see those gay little yachts and various other craft bobbing about in the creek, I know that I am really home. I have often speculated what a vast improvement it would be if the water could be kept permanently high, for at low tide the mud presents a far from attractive picture. I believe that back in the 1960s thoughts of damming the creek were mooted, but opposition from various quarters put an end to such a venture.

So much for sport on land and water, how about the high-flyers of this world? In the 20s and 30s the greatest thrill was provided by the newly-found wonders of aviation. Some readers will recall that marvellous May day in 1933 when Fareham had its very own Air Pageant, with thousands of spectators flocking to Dean Farm to view the spectacular show, the highlight being a daring display of wing-walking. By the way, profits made from this pageant were donated to the funds of Gosport War Memorial Hospital.

Of course, some folk's idea of sport is to raise a glass from counter to lips, and over the years Fareham has been able to boast a goodly number of drinking establishments. Whatever readers may feel about the evils of demon drink, or the pleasure that some derive from partaking of it, public houses and drinking dens play a strong part in the local history of any town or village. Therefore, it is a little sad that Fareham has lost several of these places of alcoholic delight in more recent times, the Travellers Rest in Wickham Road, the Chequers near the Quay, and the Rising Sun in Gosport Road being but three.

I am pleased to say that Fareham's historic coaching inn, the Red Lion, still graces the eastern end of West Street. The Hewlett family were the proprietors of this inn from the 1790s until the 1830s, and it was during this period that William Cobbett of

Rural Rides fame put up for the night there, in 1823 to be exact. During the last century the Red Lion was the scene of many colourful social functions, the grand balls held there being particularly memorable. Just imagine the scene at one such ball in 1884, 130 ladies and gentlemen of the area were assembled to dine and dance the night away, the Carpenter-Garniers of Wickham being the special guests. The music was provided by the Band of the Royal Marine Light Infantry, and the ladies in their resplendent gowns had strong competition in cutting a dash by their male partners, most of whom were wearing scarlet hunting jackets. What a marvellous sight it must have made!

Still on the subject of alcoholic lions, if you fancied a change of colour there was always the White Lion in the High Street in the last century, and of course I have already mentioned The Golden Lion in the same street. In 1870 a daring robbery was carried out at the Golden Lion, the thieves getting away with several silver plates. The Newfoundland dog that the proprietor kept in the yard for such events proved to be of little use, for the crooks had drugged it prior to the raid. In fact, they were so liberal with the dose, the poor animal slept for the whole of the following day!

For a change of animal there was the Coach and Horses in the High Street, and the White Horse, the Lamb, and the White Hart in West Street. Drinkers of a patriotic disposition might have preferred the Kings Arms or the Crown in West Street, the former has long since disappeared, but I am pleased to say that the latter is still very much in evidence. Not too far away from this part of West Street the Bugle is also still serving pints for pleasure on the corner of Quay Street, and the observant local historian will note a very interesting milestone adorning the side of this pub, it indicates that Fareham is seventy-two miles from London and five miles from the Gosport Gates.

Bearing in mind the various imports and exports that took place in the Quay area, it is not difficult to understand how the Coal Exchange derived it's name. In the last century there was a pub at Lower Quay that gets my favourite Fareham pub name award, it was called the Castle in the Air. Another name that I like is The Bird in Hand, a public house that is still going strong in nearby Gosport Road. At one time this pub was kept by a large and colourful lady named Fanny White, who was the sister of the aforementioned fishmonger Jack White, Fanny doubled as landlady and chucker-out, and believe me, when she called for drinking-up time, one did not delay!

It is difficult to imagine now that the Royal Oak on the corner of West Street and Trinity Street stands on what was formerly a pond, but that is so. Around the corner in Trinity Street we must not forget that popular little public house we knew as the Good Intent, changed in recent years to a wine bar, or the Victory Inn a little further up. Continuing on up Park Lane, or Puxol Lane if you prefer, near the top of the hill in Old Turnpike is the New Inn. It would appear that there was always a beerhouse of some kind on this site, for a lady named Hannah Dunham kept one there for many years in the last century. Hannah made her own beer on the premises, and at times she had problems with her water supply, for it was generally obtained from a nearby pond. Whenever the pond dried up she had to travel to Fontley to get water for her unique-tasting brew, although at times she employed the services of Richard Harding the local carrier to fetch it for her. Of course, the water at Fontley came from the River Meon, and I have no doubt that the Miners Arms in that fair hamlet was pleased about the close proximity of the river at times. This pub was built to supplement an earlier tavern known as the Tunnel Tavern, an establishment that derived it's name from the famous Fareham Railway Tunnel. Regular connoisseurs of ale are apt to refer to a particular brew as "Liquid Dynamite", one day in 1907 the regulars at the Miners Arms had a sample of the real thing. They were sipping quite contentedly, when suddenly the

The Alexandra, West Street.

Fareham Embassy, closed 1983.

New Inn, Old Turnpike.

Old Alexandra, 1910.

Trinity Street. Victory Inn, 1920s.

pub was severely struck by lightning, demolishing a chimney stack and stripping the roof of all its slates. Although the drinkers were thrown in all directions, I am very pleased to say that none of them were hurt, although it must have been a sad sight to see so much good ale spilt across the floor!

On the outskirts of Fareham the Old Vine is still flourishing on Crocker Hill, not many people know that this inn was once the scene of a murder that shocked the inhabitants of Fareham and Wickham. The incident took place in 1924 when the landlord was Arthur Gamblin, a gentleman who had a reputation for having a violent temper. He had in his possession a double-barrelled gun, with which he murdered his wife Sarah Jane Gamblin, his son William, his daughter Sarah, and finally he killed himself. It was not a pleasant sight for those who found the bodies. I am pleased to say that the Old Vine has settled to a peaceful existence over the past sixty years, and is still one of my favourite places for a quiet pint or two.

This Fareham pub crawl is almost developing into a book on its own, so I had better bring the subject to a close by mentioning a few more names, such as the Delme Arms, West End Inn, Railway Tavern, The Highlands, Redlands Inn, The Portland, The Toby Jug, Gordon Arms, Hoeford Inn, and the White Horse Inn and the Fort Wallington Tavern in Wallington. Yes, I know there were more, but that is all I have space for.

An excess of alcohol has been known to encourage the imbiber to sing the odd chorus or so, so we may assume that when the Fareham Glee Club met weekly at the White Horse Inn in the early 1800s, the music they produced was decidedly jolly. on the other hand, the old-established Fareham Philharmonic Society have always provided good music without the aid of alcoholic beverages. The Portland Hall provided a venue for such entertainments in days gone by, but there was also a number of other halls that resounded to the strains of music and laughter, such as the Connaught Drill Hall, the Forester's Hall, both in West Street, the British Legion or Working Mans clubs in King's Road, and the Masonic Hall in Queens Road.

If you did not fancy going out and tripping the "light fantastic", you could always put your latest 78 r.p.m. Henry Hall record on the wind-up gramophone and waltz around the kitchen pretending that Mum was really Ginger Rogers in your arms. So, whatever your fancy, leisure and pleasure is really what you make it. Unfortunately, so many folk today want to be entertained by others rather than by themselves, and have been only too ready in the past to criticize Fareham's lack of entertainment. This was answered in 1982 by the opening of the huge Ferneham Hall entertainment complex, catering for a wide variety of tastes that includes musical shows and concerts, jazz, pop, wrestling, craft and antique fairs, and much more. Also, we must not forget the Fareham & Gosport Drama Centre in Osborn Road, an excellent small theatre and workshop converted from old school buildings, where a varied and interesting programme is provided all through the year, including a season of selected films.

I just wish that I could say that Fareham still had its own cinema, but by the time, that this book reaches the public the town's last remaining picture house, the Embassy, will have closed its doors, yet another victim to the attractions of television and video. There have been three cinemas in Fareham's film history, the Alexandra 1910–33, the Savoy 1933–59, and the Embassy 1938–83. My favourite stories concern the old Alexandra in West Street, especially when it was run by the Flemon family in the 1920's. However, I do not intend to include them in this publication, for all the Fareham cinemas, and fifty others, have been covered quite extensively in *The Cinemas of Portsmouth*, another book in this series.

Open All Hours.

No **Down Memory Lane** book dealing specifically with one town or place would be complete without some mention of shops or businesses that have flourished there in bygone years, but I must admit to never knowing which way to tackle the subject, for if one should cover a particular thoroughfare such as West Street shop by shop, then only one specific year or period would be dealt with. Therefore, in order to cover as wide a span of years as possible, I will attempt to recall individual trades and traders from Fareham's past, but readers will I am sure understand that I have not enough space to include all of them.

Right, let us begin with the essentials of life, food, glorious food! Akin to most other towns, the Fareham of the 1980s is increasingly swinging over to the supermarket-style of shopping for weekly needs, thus causing the smaller grocery stores to display "Closing Down" notices. In many ways this is a great shame, for they were more than mere shops, they were meeting places where one could find out what was happening in the community. And oh! the glorious aroma that greeted one's nostrils upon entering those old grocery stores – if only they could have bottled it.

I wish that I had been around in the middle of the last century to have experienced the aromatic delights of the West Street store run by George Boorn and David Harris, for in addition to normal grocery supplies they were wine and spirit merchants, corn and coal merchants, and even included tiles and bricks in their vast quantity of stock. In many ways, Boorn & Harris were the Woolworth's of their day. In the grocery field they had strong competition from other West Street traders such as John Kennett, Henry Clark, William Cawte, James Smith, and William Matthews. Weighing packages of tea and sugar in the High Street there was John Emery and Phoebe Wrapson, whilst in Trinity Street the stores of William Binstead, William Sandy, Benjamin Talbot, and

Henry Duffett performed the same task. It would appear that down in sleepy old Wallington, the little grocery store of Elizabeth Saunders had something of a monopoly in those days.

Creeping into this century, and to within living memory, I would suspect that there are still quite a number of readers who can recall running errands for dear old Mum at grocery stores such as those run by Messrs. Horner & Munday, William Lusby, Waller & Co, Joseph Johns, Ben Tatford, Taylor & Sons, Fred Croft & Son, and Stone & Co on the corner of Trinity Street. Fareham could also boast a few national names such as Home & Colonial and the International Tea Stores, and of course we must not forget the Portsea Island Co-op.

The great advantage of being able to shop in covered precincts such as those provided in the Fareham of today, just has to be that you do not have to worry about the weather, and apart from the fact that you do not get wet, it can also be a nice place to have a free warm in the winter. Mind you, the traders of old also had a weapon against the weather elements, it was called a shop blind, and young assistants could regularly be seen struggling with these contraptions. Traders found the blinds useful for shielding their goods from the effects of the sun's rays, and also for shoppers to shelter under in the rainy season, and hopefully have time to study the magnificent display in their windows. But, I am afraid the shoppers did not always take kindly to shop blinds, for in the 1920s there were many complaints by the residents of Fareham about the dangerous obstruction caused by the blinds to pedestrians. The matter was finally resolved when the council decreed that it would be a punishable offence for shop blinds to hang less than 8ft. from the pavement.

When I think about bakers in Fareham, I invariably think of Herbert Pyle foremost. The son of a Denmead farmer, Herbert served his apprenticeship in Portsmouth for five years, following which he came to Fareham in 1883 as a partner in the confection-

Herbert Pyle's Paragon Bakery.

Abraham's High Street Emporium.

Mr. Collins, the High Street Butcher.

Bunney's Boot Repair Shop, Gosport Road.

Sid Fry working in Job's Jewellers Shop, 1930s.

1912.

ery business of his uncle, Mr. W. Pyle. Herbert branched out on his own in later years, buying the old Paragon Hotel premises in West Street, and converting it into a bakery that he named the Paragon Bakery. By the way, this was formerly the site of the White Hart inn. Anyhow, Herbert Pyle's bakery venture was a huge success, and he was soon in a position to open other branches. In the pre 1914–18 war years there was also a temperance and commercial hotel in West Street that sported the name of Pyle. This master baker also served on the urban district council for some years, filling one term as Chairman.

Bakery names from the last century include those of George Pink, Edward Smith, Robert Coker, George Young, Jeremiah Bachelo, Richard Edwards, and John Pannell. Then in later years, Stephen Hales, William Wills, Price Brothers, and Smith & Vosper, were all in West Street, whilst kneading and needing the dough in Gosport Road there was Hobden & Son next to the Rising Sun.

Do you remember when dinner plates were overlapped with meat? When Dad came home from work and sat down for his evening meal, he always used to loosen off his belt first in anticipation of what he was about to receive! Those were the days, and the meat really tasted like meat, no frozen delights then! Never mind, I have begun fattening-up our canary for next Christmas!

Fareham's chief butchers in the town of the last century included Joseph Daysh and John Emery in the High Street, William Daysh, Edmund Cawte, and Charles Howard in West Street, and Mary Coker and Henry Duffett in Trinity Street. Then wielding the meat axe in the early years of this century was George Burt in East Street at No. 2., whilst in nearby West Street there was John Adams, Frank Bussey, Eastmans, Dewhurst, William Wood, Henry Hayward, the London Central Meat Company, William Pink, and everyone's favourite pork butcher, Albert Shepherd near the bus station. The name of Burt still flourishes in

East Street, as does Mr. Collins' well-known establishment in the High Street. Alas, Arthur North's butchers shop in Gosport Road is no longer with us.

How about some nice fresh vegetables to go with your meat? Eager to serve with scales and scoop at the ready were Roland Trigg, George Rampton, George Baker, E. Hills, Martin Pyle, and Horace Craven. Lovers of fish were well catered for by Tom Cripps, George Walters, George Ward, and not forgetting the aforementioned Jack White with his speedy donkey-cart. On the other hand, like myself, some folks preferred their fish and chips out of a newspaper, and battling with the batter was Alf Spender in West Street, Fred Dady in Gosport Road, and Fred and John Meek in Trinity Street.

To complete our look back at food establishments, I will remind readers of some of the town's old dairy shops. I have already mentioned our old farmer friend Tom Parker, and also filling the milk jugs were Holliday & Sons, William Sear, Henry Pink, and William Goodenough. And that is where we must take our minds away from food, and on to what are known in the retail trade as dry goods.

There are still probably quite a number of Fareham folk who will recall buying their very first bedroom suite or table and chairs in that renowned furnishing emporium run by the Abraham family in the High Street. If this store did not have in stock what the customer wanted, then it would have been very surprising, for Abraham's operated as furnishers and cabinet makers, china dealers, wine merchants, auctioneers, valuers, and estate agents. The business was started by Edmund Abraham in 1827, and eventually passed into the hands of his son William, whose wife Catherine also took an active part in the running of the store. The family carried on the name when William died in 1907, followed by Catherine in 1926. A few years after her death the family suffered a tragic loss, this happened in 1929 when George

Abraham was cleaning a double barrelled shotgun at his Hill Head home, it went off, discharging a shot through George's head and killing him instantly. The High Street furnishing store was taken over by Pilcher & Co., Mr. C.E. Pilcher also being connected with the renowned Gosport furnishing firm of Hoare & Pilcher.

Abraham's also had a store known as the "Little Dustpan" near the bus station in West Street, and this was taken over later by another well known Fareham furnishing family, W.H. Jeffery & Sons. It all began when William Jeffery opened a small shop in Trinity Street in 1903, and William was also fortunate in having a good partner in business and life, for his wife Kate was a very shrewd and commercially-minded lady.

Charlie May had his cycle business next to Abraham's in the High Street for many years. A progressive sort of a chap, Charlie was quick to supplement his bicycles with motor cycles when they became popular after the First World War, then when the wireless age came into our homes in the early 20s, he was one of the first dealers in Fareham to sell radio receivers. May's suffered quite a big setback in 1928 when the High Street shop caught fire, and although Arthur Sutton and his brave lads were on the scene within five minutes, over £1,000 of damage was caused. Charlie's biggest cycle dealer rival in the High Street was the aforementioned Hansford's, but not very far away in West Street there was another flourishing cycle concern in the form of Grafham & Sons, who also operated as motor engineers near the old fire station. My old friend Betty Grafham once showed me an amazing family picture taken in the early years of this century, it shows the Grafham boys riding a remarkable bicycle built for four riders, built in the West Street workshop. Unfortunately, the photograph is in rather poor condition, so I am unable to reproduce it in these pages, but I am pleased to be able to mention this old Fareham establishment. But my final word on bicycles must go to the Fareham Cycle Works, which was in fact sited in the High Street on the same site as Charlie May in even earlier days. This business was under the proprietorship of the Hunt family, and in large letters on the fascia of their shop they proudly proclaimed that they were the makers of the famous Swallow bicycle.

Next door, on the corner of the High Street and West Street, stood the drapery and millinery emporium of Montague Warn, the ideal place to purchase elastic for ladies unmentionables. This desirable site was taken over in later years by draper Frank Kemp, then by the 1930s it was in the hands of Brighter Homes, the wallpaper and paint retailers. Fareham could boast several drapery establishments in the old days, but I think that the foremost name just has to be that of Albion Dodge & Son. What a wonderfully quaint old place this West Street store was, long and narrow with a selection of various departments dealing in materials, outfitting, and footwear. The quality and cost of their goods were always good and reasonable, hence the regular parade of farm workers who would invade the Dodge premises on market days, their main objective being the tough working shirts and boots that were generally in stock. Dodge's had one of those marvellous overhead cash conveyance systems that I have written about many times in this local history series, and whereas these tracks were fairly plentiful in places such as Portsmouth and Gosport, the system was not widely used in Fareham. When the time came for Albion Dodge to go to the "Great Draper in the Sky", the drapery and outfitting store was taken over by William Dodge. Alas, this revered establishment no longer exists, and one cannot purchase a vest and knicker set for 5/11d., or a pair of strong boots for five bob. Mind you, I would look pretty silly strolling down West Street only dressed in vest, knickers, and boots! On the other hand, compared with some of the punk creations that haunt the Fareham Precinct on Saturday afternoons, I would probably pass for normal! My final word on

William Jeffery outside his furnishing store in Trinity Street, 1918.

Baker's, the West Street Greengrocers.

Gosport Road Garage, demolished 1980.

Fareham Steam Laundry, Gosport Road.

Spencer Lamb, Newsagent. Now Bartlett's.

Old Wallington.

West Street, Savoy Buildings.

White Horse, Wallington.

drapers goes to a store that was but a few door away from Dodge's in West Street, the old established concern of Matthew Letheren, where one was always met with a fixed smile and an ever- ready tape measure, which has to be an improvement on the vacant stare that one receives from shop assistants today.

Every town or city appears to specialize in a particular trade or commodity, for instance, Portsmouth at one time could definitely be classed as one of the chief centres in the country for the corset-making industry. Regarding Fareham, the main trade seems to have been boot and shoe manufacturing, for there were more of these establishments than food supply shops. The White's Directory of 1859 lists no fewer than fifteen boot and shoe makers, and in the early part of this century there were more than that. One of the more familiar Fareham names that is included in the 1859 list is that of John Privett in West Street, which even then had been in existence about fifty years. This family business eventually passed to Charles Privett, who carried out his tapping and hammering in Gosport Road. In the tradition of his father and grandfather before him, Charles was renowned for the heavy water boots that he made for farmers and seamen, and for over 25 years he had a contract with Fareham U.D.C. to supply footwear for their workers. Away from his workbench he was a bellringer at the parish church for fifty years, and it was through his efforts that new bells were installed in 1883 to complete the octave. Charles died in 1925 aged 80, and his wife Fanny followed him some 12 years later, leaving four sons and two daughters. His eldest son, George Privett, was well known for his knowledge on local history, writing the popular "Historicus" column in the *Hampshire Telegraph*, which led to one of the few books written about the town, namely *The Story of Fareham* in 1949.

Another much respected name in the Fareham footwear world was that of Leo Sturgess, and when he died in 1980 at the age of 82 it was believed that he was the last hand-sewn boot and shoe maker in the town. Operating from a workshop in the garden of his Osborn Road home, Leo began his business in 1919, specializing in made-to-measure boots and shoes. Such was the fame of his work, customers came from all over Hampshire. Leo's house and place of work overlook the churchyard of S.S. Peter & Paul, so it is fitting that there is a memorial stone to him in those quiet and tranquil grounds. I cannot mention all of them, but here are a few cobbling names from the past, George Kiddle, Henry Reed, George Corbin, Edward Martell, Tom Pullen, George Oliver, Charles Chase, Henry Dicker, Frank Spencer, and James Cecil Bunney, who took over Privett's old shop in Gosport Road.

The world of commerce has always relied heavily on the power of the printed word, a statement that the family printing business of Hector Duffett in the High Street would readily substantiate, for I am pleased to say that this old-established concern is still flourishing in the 1980s. In the early 1900s Duffett's published an excellent series of picture postcards relating to Fareham, as did another old printing firm in West Street, Sutton & Sons. They also dealt in books, stationery, and newspapers. The latter were also supplied by newsagent Spencer Lamb, whose shop was sited near the old Alexandra Cinema. The name changed in later years to Lamb & Coleborn, and later still to Messrs. Bartlett & Sons, another popular newsagent and tobacconists where the reader may have purchased this book. Another shop nearby where cinema-goers may have got there sweets or fags before sampling the delights of Charlie Chaplin or Rin-Tin-Tin was the shop of William Worley, whose son Jim actually worked in the cinema as a projectionist, and subsequently married Miss Guy in the ticket office. They did not get married in the actual ticket office of course, she only worked there!

William Worley also carried out a spot of hairdressing in his time, but "The" name in Fareham's world of comb and scissor merchants just has to be that of Knipe & Sons, who have (and still do) perform a countless number of "short, back, and sides" operations. In earlier days, George Hoare on the corner of Adelaide Place, Len Grafham in West Street, or Walter Cooper in the High Street, were all pretty nifty with the haircutting tools. The latter gentleman, Walter John Cooper, later had his name over a tobacco and confectionery supply business in the High Street, which only closed in recent times.

In the old days it was always fashionable to strut around the town with a watch dangling on a chain across your waistcoat, and supplying that particular piece of "old iron" Fareham had a good selection of jewellers, names such as William Vimpany, Arthur Weeks, Charles Robinson, and Harold Job. Mention of the latter shop reminds me that my old friend Sid Fry once worked in Mr. Job's West Street store in the 1930s. Sid also has fond memories of his boyhood in the Gosport Road area of the town, a good part of which has now vanished in the cause of road widening.

All books in the **Down Memory Lane** series contain a good selection of old photographs within their pages, and I am particularly grateful that photographers such as F.G.O. Stuart of Southampton, William Smith of Gosport, and A.H. Sweasey of Southsea managed to visit the Fareham of yesteryear. But on the home front there have also been a number of skilled picture-takers to record the town's ever-changing face, names such as Frank Pannell, Sidney Smith, and J.T. See. The latter, whose full name was Joseph Thurston See, was noted for his fine portrait work, and had his premises in West Street on the corner of Hartlands Road. Until his death in 1907 he was also one of Fareham's most prominent men, serving nine years on the urban district council, including a term as Chairman, and was also one of the founders of Fareham Sailing Club. Mr. See's photographic work is particularly collectable, for he began clicking in Fareham in 1887.

If all this name-dropping has given you a headache, it certainly has me, then I would suggest a visit to the chemist's shop, but alas, names such as Egbert Neville and Batchelors in West Street no longer exist. Of course, there are illnesses that headache powders will not cure, and this leads us to the last trade of this section, undertakers. This occupation usually goes hand in hand with buildings or cabinet-makers, and the Fareham undertaking concerns of Ewart Moss and Michael Coghlan are no exception. The Coghlan story is another case of a tradesman having good support from his wife, for Michael and Anne Coghlan celebrated their golden wedding in 1912 with their five sons.

I could seemingly go on and on with this subject, but lack of space is one of my constant enemies, so please do not write and tell me that I did not mention your old Uncle Fred who had a sweet-shop in West Street. On the other hand, I have somehow managed to include well over one hundred names in this section.

The Last Word.

That concludes our journey back to *The Fareham of Yesteryear*, I sincerely hope that it has afforded readers pleasure, and that they deem it good value for money. Although I have touched upon Wallington, Fontley, and Peel Common, I have deliberately refrained from including Titchfield, Portchester, or Stubbington, the reason being that they really warrant individual books, also when one buys a book on Fareham, then it should concentrate on Fareham.

How about the Fareham of today? To anyone who resides in or has visited the town in recent years, it will be obvious that great changes have been made, and are still being made. Fareham's huge modern shopping precinct is now a formidable rival to the formerly dominant commercial centres of Portsmouth and Southampton, and complements the giant civic office buildings and associated departments. Not forgetting the excellent town library, and the aforementioned Ferneham Hall entertainment complex. The feed and ring road systems are currently being improved in the Gosport Road and Quay areas, and we have the prospect of a fly-over at the Delme Roundabout to look forward to, thus, hopefully, easing the traffic situation.

With all these changes, it is vital that local historians should make a photographic record for future generations, for if chaps such as See, Pannell, Smith, Sweasey, and Stuart had not done so in the past, it would be difficult to illustrate books such as this. We may be glad that in the Fareham Local History Group we have a band of dedicated enthusiasts who are determined to preserve the town's historical heritage, and if my humble efforts have evoked a measure of interest for the reader, I would suggest that they would do well to join this group, or to regularly subscribe to their publication *Fareham Past & Present*. The Local History Group also hopes that one day the town will have its own museum, a project that will I am sure be supported by the residents, for Fareham has plenty of history that should be preserved.

North Hill.

Fareham Road, Catisfield.

Old Turnpike Post Office.

Price's School, 1930s.

The Golden Lion.

Quay Road improvement scheme, 1982.

Old Fareham Fire Station and Parish Hall.